THE SINGER'S MANUAL
of ENGLISH DICTION

by

MADELEINE MARSHALL

Instructor in English Diction
Juilliard School of Music
School of Sacred Music, Union Theological Seminary

X–218

G. SCHIRMER
New York / London

CONTENTS

PART I

                                                                        Page

1. Conference 1
2. Silent Letters (Spelled but not Sounded) 6
3. Division of Syllables 7
4. *r:* The Two Kinds 8
5. The Three Basic Rules for Omitting and Sounding *r* . . 9
6. Which Kind of *r* to Sing Before a Vowel 16
7. *y:* Sometimes a Consonant, Sometimes a Vowel 27
8. Voiceless and Voiced Consonants 29
9. *t* and *d* 32
10. Lip Consonants 40
11. Lip Consonants: *p* and *b* 41
12. Lip Consonants: *f* and *v* 48
13. *m* and *n* 56
14. When to Separate Words 64
15. *l* 68
16. *k* and "Hard" *g* 74
17. Final *b*, *d*, and "Hard" *g* 80
18. *th* 87
19. Additional Instructions About *r* 95
20. *ng* [ŋ] 98
21. *h* 101
22. *wh* and *w* 103
23. *s* and *z* 107
24. *s* and *z* for Those who Lisp 109
25. *sh* and [ʒ] 115
26. *ch* and "Soft" *g* or *j* 117

		Page
27.	Summary of Connections	120
28.	Summary of Special Directions for Incidental Words	121

PART II

29.	Vowels; Phonetic Alphabet	122
30.	[ɑ] as in Father (We Call it *Ah*)	125
31.	[ɛ] as in Wed	127
32.	[ɪ] as in It	129
33.	[i] as in Me	131
34.	[æ] as in Cat	133
35.	[u] as in Too	136
36.	Daniel Sitteth	139
37.	[ʊ] as in Full	142
38.	[o] as in Obey	143
39.	[ɔ] as in Warm	144
40.	[ɜ] as in Learn	146
41.	[ʌ] as in Up	148
42.	[ə]: The Neutral Vowel	150
43.	Unstressed Syllables that Do Not Have the Neutral Vowel	156
44.	[a], [ɒ], [e]: Why We Do Not Sing Them	163
45.	Diphthongs	165
46.	The First Five Diphthongs as in Night, Day, Boy, Now, No	167
47.	Diphthongs and Triphthongs Ending in the Neutral Vowel as in Air, Ear, Ire, Ore, Sure, Our	174
48.	When to Sing [æ]; When to Sing *Ah*	185
49.	To Rhyme or Not to Rhyme	192
50.	A Last Word: Patter	194
	Appendix 1	196
	Appendix 2	198

Part I

1. CONFERENCE

We are starting a series of lessons about English diction, and before the singing begins, let's have a little friendly gossip about singers. There are five principal objectives in this manual, and a cheerful way to outline them is to discuss types of vocalists whose diction has prevented them from reaching these objectives. You and I have listened to such singers, and as we share our genial recollections of their shortcomings, we shall arrive at the general bases for our work.

Just before we review our first group of singers, we'll try to define what diction is. There are many definitions, and perhaps a full-dress statement is superfluous anyhow. However that may be, we may take "diction" to mean one word, and that word is "words."

We have heard singers whose English couldn't be understood because they distorted the words beyond recognition. There are some familiar expressions that describe this sort of enunciation: "He (or she) sings as if he had a hot potato in his mouth . . . as if he had a mouthful of mush . . . as if his mouth were full of marbles." One of the purposes of this manual is to help singers remove potatoes, mush, and marbles from their songs in English. It may, coincidentally, be of casual service in improving clarity in other languages, but it's a book about singing in English and isn't intended as a guide to anything else.

You and I have attended musical sessions at which many of the words were clear — but they weren't the words that the poet had written. Careless or mannered pronunciation has brought to audiences such unconventional declarations as "I swallow my bride,"

1

"I am yawning for your love," "I hear you hauling me," "I am the master of my feet," "I am wading for you," and "sea nymphs sourly ring his knell." The catalogue of such blops, as they are known informally, could extend this book alarmingly. We shall encounter many of them as we go from chapter to chapter, ranging from such innocent peccadilloes as the spearmint error ("Nymphs and shepherds, gum away") to such obvious breaches of decorum as "Let us sin." This manual has been devised to assist the singer in avoiding misunderstandings, in all senses of that word.

We have been auditors of singers who sang with so much physical pressure that they squeezed the words into senselessness. Clear singing is easy singing. And one of the greatest pleasures in my years of teaching has been to hear singers observe that the clarification of their diction has been helpful in effecting vocal relaxation and tonal improvement. At this point, I'd like to make it plain that this book is not a treatise on voice building or tone production. I have never masterminded a voice teacher or interfered with his work on the singer's voice. The counsel and cooperation of voice teachers have been of great value to me, and it has been gratifying to learn from them that this study of diction has been a useful supplement to their own instruction. There can hardly be disagreement on the fundamental truth that the most beautiful consonants and vowels are those that are pronounced with complete relaxation of the lips and the throat muscles.

Have you heard concerted music — anything from a duet to an opera or an oratorio — in which there were wonderfully varied pronunciations of the same word by different singers? I can recall an opera in English where five characters, in turn, sang the word *water*. What came out was "wawter, wahter, wawter, wahter, wawter." You might well hear a performance in which the same episode brought forth "wawter, wahter, wutter, watter, wawder," or at least a half dozen other pronunciations of H_2O. This disparity in pronunciation is disconcerting to an audience. There is a temptation to compile many examples, but we'll add only one here: a quartet, which, singing the ecstatic word, *rapture,* offers in musical but not verbal harmony, "raptyoor," "ratcher," "rahpture," and "rupture." Here we have four simultaneous interpretations of the same word. They have one thing in common: they are all incorrect.

In this manual, there is presented a neutral, standard English, free of regional accents, intelligible to any audience. It is an English that has long been accepted as a norm on the stage and in other public usage. The recommendation of this English for singing is, of course, no criticism of the English spoken in any given area. Our aim is to sing one English. If this standard pronunciation differs from your speech at home, don't worry! Your personal speech is your own prerogative, like your preference in clothing. (I may as well confess that my own patois usually tells visitors that I grew up in the north of New York State.) But just as there is an integration of costuming on the stage, so is there a necessary unifying of pronunciation in music — and this doesn't apply only to English!

We've talked about clarity, accuracy, ease, and uniformity in the singing of English. A fifth important objective is expressiveness. You've heard note-perfect and production-perfect singers who communicated nothing to their listeners because they ejected the words in the manner of automatons, ma king ev e ry syl la ble stand out sep a rate ly. Such vocalists are accused of being "cold," "insensitive," or "monotonous," although they may be sizzling with internal emotion. In this manual, you will find many specific devices for conveying expressiveness through diction.

*   *

*

Here is a little shop talk about some of the things you will and will not find in this book. It may be useful to have in mind as you proceed to the rules, the drills, and the suggestions.

There are many examples from vocal literature to illustrate the treatment of consonants and vowels. I have chosen these excerpts principally on the basis of their frequent appearances in my classes. When a piece of music is brought in again and again by students from many parts of the country, students from a large variety of voice teachers, it may be assumed that this composition is familiar and available to most singers. If you happen not to know the setting for the texts that are quoted, you may practice the words on any notes that you care to choose. The use of a known setting is usually preferable to impromptu composition, but you can become acquainted with the principle involved even when you don't happen to be acquainted with the music to which the words are most frequently sung. There has been no attempt to limit any quotation to any one appearance. Some texts are unusually fertile in illustrative material, which is a convenience to the singer as well as to the compiler. There are no reproductions of the settings, because the accumulation of

musical examples would add greatly to the bulk of the volume —
and to the costs for the publisher and for the reader!

I hope that this manual will remain in your library — or in an
even more accessible place — for reference after you have studied
it through. Because of the reference possibilities, it has been divided
into two parts: consonants and vowels. But when you work with the
manual for the first time, the best procedure is to alternate consonant
sections and vowel sections.

Why does it begin with consonants? Because singers vocalize on
vowels. This isn't intended as "a most ingenious paradox." You are
already familiar with vowels as an independent element in your
singing, but you may not have heard so much about consonants and
their importance. They project the voice. They focus it. They en-
hance its volume. They supply carrying power. They are as vital
to singing an effective pianissimo as in creating a stirring fortissimo.

You will find phonetic symbols in the course of these lessons.
These excellent aids are employed only when they provide the most
concise identification of a sound. You won't see many of them in
the consonant chapters, but they are well in evidence in the vowel
sections. If you've studied phonetics, of course you know them as
old and welcome friends; if you haven't, you will get on good terms
with them as you study the vowels. The symbols are enclosed in
square brackets to distinguish them from conventional spelling.

You will, I hope, pardon me if I make an observation on the
style in which this manual is written. I've tried to set down, with
reasonable brevity, the many principles, devices, and suggestions that
have been developed in my teaching and coaching of singing in
English at the Juilliard School of Music, the Union Theological
Seminary, the Metropolitan Opera, and network programs, as well
as in private work with singers, including many eminent artists. The
rules and their accessories are the results of what has been taught
and tried for some twenty years. I might have enjoyed writing them
up with more graceful flourishes, but I'm not, by profession, an
author, and I've tried simply to make everything clear and practical.

Acknowledgments are always in order when a book based on
experience comes to print. A complete roster of those who have, in
many different ways, stimulated and inspired me, would include the
names of hundreds of singers, of scores of teachers, composers, and
conductors. It is only for the sake of space that they remain name-
less here. They will understand, I know, if I make an exception for

Mack Harrell, who, both as singing artist and as teacher, has tested and checked and re-checked many of the principles that appear in the manual, and has served as an endlessly amiable, efficient, and constructive human laboratory for research in the sound of our language.

With which we'll start singing.

2. SILENT LETTERS

(SPELLED, BUT NOT SOUNDED)

Many English words include letters that are not sounded, but are present only because the language is not always pronounced as it is spelled. For our purposes, we shall consider these non-sounded letters as non-existent. Throughout this manual, the word "vowel" or "consonant" means a vowel or consonant that is sounded. These words never apply to silent letters. The disregard of silent letters is an important principle whose application will become increasingly apparent in the course of this book.

Consider one of the most valuable verbs: *are*. In practical use, it is a two-letter word: *ar*. The *e* is part of the spelling but not part of the sound, and, because it is not sounded, we sing the word as if it contained no *e* at any time. In diction, the word ends in the consonant *r*.

More examples:

The final *e* in *where* and *there* is silent. Therefore, these words end in a consonant.

The *h* in *hour* and *honor* is silent. Therefore, these words begin with a vowel sound.

The *w* in *write* and *wrong* is silent. Therefore, these words begin with *r*.

The *k* in *know* and *knew* is silent. Therefore, these words begin with *n*.

SOME CONSONANTS SOUNDED, BUT NOT SPELLED

There are also a few words in which a consonant is sounded, but not spelled. For example, in the word *one*, pronounced *won*, the *w* is not present in the spelling, but is sounded. In practice, *one* actually begins with a consonant.

More examples:

The word *once* is pronounced *wonce*. Therefore it begins with a consonant.

The words *union* and *united* are pronounced *yunion* and *yunited*. Therefore they begin with a consonant.

6

3. DIVISION OF SYLLABLES

The conventional printed division of words into syllables does not necessarily coincide with the division of syllables in song. A word of two or more syllables is divided, in print, on the basis of its structure; the same word, when sung, may be divided in an entirely different manner for the sake of clearer and more effective singing.

The vocal treatment of syllables will be explained with the study of individual consonants; the following examples are intended merely to illustrate variations between divisions in print and in song:

Division of syllables printed under notes	Division of syllables when sung
spir-it-u-al	*spi-ri-tu-al*
seat-ed	*sea-ted*
dif-fer-ence	*di-ffe-rence*
re-mind-er	*rem-in-der*
a-noint	*an-oint*

THE HYPHEN IS NOT A REST

Here is a warning about that useful typographical device, the hyphen (-), which is employed universally to indicate the division of syllables: do not interpret it, musically, as a rest. It does not indicate an interruption in the flow of music.

SUSTAINING OF VOWELS

Some singers unconsciously place an unauthorized rest between a vowel and a consonant that are to be joined. They permit the vowel to die into complete silence before sounding the consonant. Such a breaking up of word or phrase is neither good sense nor good singing. The vowel must be sustained until the consonant takes over.

7

4. *r:* THE TWO KINDS

Although there are some curious theories about the singing of *r*, in our work we shall limit the pronunciation to two varieties. Each of these has specific uses which will presently be discussed in detail. By way of preliminary, we shall define the two *r*'s:

1. The American *r*.
2. The flipped *r*.

1. The American *r*. This is the conventional term generally used to designate the *r* most prevalent in American speech — the *r* we employ in our daily conversation. It is sounded while turning the tip of the tongue upward in the direction of, but not touching, the back of the upper gum ridge, and returning it to its original position.

2. The flipped *r*. "Flipped" is a term we have devised as a convenient word to designate the *r* that is most prevalent in England. It is sounded while flipping the tip of the tongue against the upper gum ridge. The tongue actually touches the gum ridge once — and only once. Imagine an Englishman saying "very sorry" and you have the flipped *r*. The tongue should flip against the gum only once, even when singing a word spelled with double *r* (*sorry, morrow,* etc.).

If you cannot flip an *r*, try this exercise: repeat *veddy, veddy, veddy* many times as rapidly as possible. Eventually *veddy* will become *very* with a flipped *r*. Follow the same procedure with *soddy, soddy, soddy* (*sorry*). Continue your practice with the following words, substituting *d* for *r*, and maintaining a good prestissimo:

bury	borrow
carry	morrow
hurry	marry

Do not expand the single flip of the tongue into two or more flips. This would result in a rolled or trilled *r*, which is inappropriate and undesirable in standard English. It is suitable only in a few specialized dialects.

5. THE THREE BASIC RULES FOR OMITTING AND SOUNDING *r*

1. Never Sing *r* Before A Consonant. (No exceptions.)
   (This rule remains in effect whether the *r* and following consonant are within the same word or in adjoining words of the same phrase.)
2. Do Not Sing *r* Before A Pause. (One exception.)
3. Always Sing *r* Before A Vowel Sound. (No exceptions.)
   (This rule remains in effect whether the *r* and following vowel sound are within the same word or in adjoining words of the same phrase.)

These rules apply to all types of music, from the most formal oratorio to the most informal popular song. The kind of *r* to be used under Rule 3 will vary, and this will be discussed fully in our next chapter. But the omission or inclusion of *r* given in the three basic rules above remains constant, always.

There is no change in the vowel sound. When *r* is omitted, the syllable must have the same vowel sound that it would have had if the *r* had not been omitted.

FIRST BASIC RULE OF *r:* Never Sing *r* Before a Consonant.

This is a rule with no exceptions, a rare circumstance in the English language, which, to some observers, seems to have more exceptions than rules.

To illustrate this important rule in action, try the following experiment: sing the word *charm* in three ways — first with an American *r*, then with a flipped *r*, and finally with no *r* at all (*chahm*). By comparing these three pronunciations, it becomes obvious that the last is the most euphonious and natural. The American *r*, when sung before a consonant, gives the voice an unpleasant, snarling

9

sound. The vowel preceding the *r* is altered by the upward turning of the tongue and seems to be chewed. When the flipped *r* is sung before a consonant, the effect is of some foreign accent or of that strange dialect known as "Singers' English," an artificiality and distortion with which no artist ought to traffic. It has been said that people never pronounce *r* this way — only singers!

When the *r* before a consonant is omitted, the vowel that precedes it has comparatively much greater purity, clarity, and beauty. The word or phrase does not lose understandability; on the contrary, its intelligibility is increased, because the consonant stands out more clearly and is all the easier to articulate when *r* is no longer an impediment. English, sung in this way, is a truly musical language.

Try the above experiment with other words, such as *garden, morning, heart, Lord, bird, mercy, warm, there.*

When the *r* is omitted, some of you will say, "I hear an *r*." But you only imagine that you hear it because you have seen the *r* on paper.

In some instances, as in the words *there* and *here,* the *r* that you will think you hear is not an *r*, but the second vowel of a diphthong. (Two vowels in the same syllable are called a diphthong; in the words now under discussion, the first vowel merges into an obscured second sound which is called the neutral vowel.) Diphthongs will be fully discussed in Part II of this manual. At present, we merely list a few examples:

their	here	more	sure
there	dear	fore	poor
fair	cheer	door	tour

The *r* should be omitted whether it occurs before a consonant in the same word or in an adjoining word of the same phrase. For example: *summer day* is pronounced *summe' day, for me* is *faw me, a star shines* is *a stah shines.*

DO NOT SHORTEN WORD IN WHICH *r* IS OMITTED

When *r* is omitted, some singers have a tendency to shorten the word by singing the final consonant too early. This results in a change of the meaning of the word. For instance, the premature singing of *k* in *Hark! hark! the lark* results in *Hock! hock! the lock.* If you have been accustomed to singing *r* where it should be omitted, simply

prolong the vowel sound to take up the time formerly occupied by *r*. To illustrate: sing *Hahk! hahk! the lahk.*
More examples:

heart is sung as *haht*, not *hot*
dark is sung as *dahk*, not *dock*
part is sung as *paht*, not *pot*

(It is curious how the undue shortening of a vowel often can change a romantic word into something prosaic.)

Practice singing the following words and phrases without an *r* (we have placed a line through every *r* that is to be omitted):

chaɍm	foɍ me	meɍcy	sailoɍ songs
gaɍden	summeɍ day	waɍm	winteɍ stoɍms
moɍning	staɍ shines	foɍget	faɍ flung
heaɍt	heɍ voice	foɍgive	otheɍ thoughts
Loɍd	theiɍ sisteɍs	peɍhaps	undeɍ skies
biɍd	eveɍ faithful	foɍloɍn	neveɍ paɍted

Foɍ behold, daɍkness shall coveɍ the eaɍth. (*Messiah;* Handel)

O heaɍ me, Loɍd, and answeɍ me; and show this people that Thou aɍt Loɍd God; and let theiɍ heaɍts again be tuɍned.

(*Elijah;* Mendelssohn)

r BEFORE SILENT LETTERS

In Chapter 2 we discussed the principle that silent letters (letters spelled but not sounded) do not exist in pronunciation. Therefore, an *r* before a silent letter is governed by whatever follows the silent letter. When a consonant follows, the *r* is omitted.

For example: *You are mine.* The *e* in *are* is silent (*arҽ*). Therefore, the *r* is followed by the consonant *m* in *mine,* and should be omitted. The phrase is sung: *You ah mine.*

In the phrases below, we have placed a line through both the *r* and the silent letter.
Practice singing:

A last faɍewell.	Faɍe thee well.
We aɍe sad.	Wheɍe does he dwell.
Befoɍe night falls . . .	Oh, come let us adoɍe Him.
I theɍefoɍe say to thee . . . (*Elijah;* Mendelssohn)	

Theɍe weɍe shepheɍds abiding in the field, keeping watch oveɍ theiɍ flocks by night.   (*Messiah;* Handel)

If shoɍt my Span I less can spaɍe
To pass a single Pleasure by . . . (Air from *Comus;* Milton, Arne)

r BEFORE A CONSONANT THAT IS SOUNDED, BUT NOT SPELLED

In Chapter 2 we discussed words in which a consonant not present in the spelling is sounded. We mentioned the word *one*, which is pronounced *won*, and therefore begins with a consonant. In a phrase such as *for one*, the *r* is followed by the consonant *w*, and is omitted. This phrase is sung: *for won*.
Practice singing:

    for once (for wonce)   *for union (for yunion)*
    we are one (we are won)   *we are united (we are yunited)*

r BEFORE r

When a word ending in *r* is followed by a word beginning with *r*, only the second *r* is sounded.
Examples:

    her riches   *other realms*   *we are ready (we ah ready)*

SECOND BASIC RULE OF *r:* Do Not Sing *r* Before a Pause.

"Before a pause" requires a bit of definition. We use this term for convenience to designate any place where you come to a stop: to take a breath; for interpretative punctuation which may clarify the text; because the composer has inserted a rest; or for special emphasis. When, for any of these reasons, you have come to a stop, omit the *r* for good tone and naturalness. Try the phrase *Oh, shining star!* in three styles: with the American *r*, the flipped *r*, and with no *r* whatever. In the first method, the word *star* sounds masticated; and in the second, the *r* imparts a foreign accent. The third method sounds most pleasing, with no sacrifice of clarity.
Practice singing:

    Oh, shining star!   —whoever they are —
    . . . when life is over;   . . . each melodious measure.
    . . . echoing from afar.   . . . for my mother (𝄽)
    Have you felt the wool of beaver, —
    Or swan's down ever? (*Have You Seen But a White Lily Grow;*
                                  Ben Jonson)
    No flow'r could be sweeter,
    No form could be neater . . . (*Clorinda;* Bledlowe, Morgan)
    From there (𝄽) it comes to kiss baby's eyes.
        (*The Sleep That Flits on Baby's Eyes;* Tagore, Carpenter)

EXCEPTION

There is one exception which will be recorded here briefly, but studied later on:

When a diphthong (as in *dear*) or a triphthong (as in *fire*) is followed by a pause on one of your highest tones, it will be more satisfactory to flip the *r*. (This exception will be described in detail on pp. 183-84 in Chapter 47, which is devoted to diphthongs and triphthongs.)

NO BAD SOCIAL CONSEQUENCES

Occasionally one encounters a student who fears that the omission of *r* will subject him to charges of affectation. If you should happen to suffer from such misgivings, please abandon them now. The omission of *r*, as described in these pages, is part of what is called Standard English — the pronunciation of platform, stage, screen, and loudspeaker. Audiences throughout the country, no matter what their own regional accents may be, are so accustomed to hearing it as transmitted by cinema, radio, and television that they take it for granted.

Even though, in your conversation with family and friends, your speech will rightly remain just as it was — like theirs — they will not observe any change when you sing with this pronunciation, and it will seem completely natural to their ears, because of its prevalent usage in public performances.

And many singers will testify that the omission of *r* is of vocal benefit.

THIRD BASIC RULE OF *r*: Always Sing *r* Before a Vowel.

It is now apparent that there is only one situation where *r* is sung: before a vowel. And here it cannot be omitted. There are no exceptions. This is true whether the *r* is followed by a vowel within the same word or in adjoining words of the same phrase. (Examples: *spirit, for us.*)

Without an *r*, such words or phrases could not be understood.
    spirit would sound like *spit*
    arise would sound like *eyes*
    pray would sound like *pay*

sorrow would sound like *sow*
wrote would sound like *oat*
for us would sound like *fuss* (approximately)
far away would sound like nothing intelligible

Reminder: The word "vowel" means a vowel that is sounded. It does not apply to a silent letter.

SING LEGATO

The clearest way to sing words is to sing them legato. Staccato singing has its value for special effects, but most of song is musicalized speech. When we speak, we do not se par ate ev er y syl la ble, but link each syllable to the next. This should also be done in singing. Of course, words are not to be mushed together; they must be joined skillfully. The legato principle underlies the *r* connection we are about to study.

HOW TO CONNECT *r* WITH FOLLOWING SYLLABLE OR WORD

When *r* is followed by a vowel sound in the next syllable, sing the *r* as the beginning of the next syllable, in this direction (→), no matter how the word may be divided in print. Example: *spir-it* should be sung as *spi-rit*.

Similarly, when *r* is followed by a vowel sound in the next word, sing the *r* as the beginning of the next word, in this direction (→). Example: *for us* should be sung as *fo-rus*.

As we said in Chapter 3, the use of the hyphen does not indicate a rest. Here, it merely demonstrates that the *r* starts the second syllable or word. In fact, the *r* is used as a connecting link, a liaison, binding the two syllables or words together in a smooth legato.

Practice singing the following words and phrases, first with an American *r*, then with a flipped *r*.

spirit	(*spi-rit*)	for us	(*fo-rus*)
arise	(*a-rise*)	near it	(*nea-rit*)
dearest	(*dea-rest*)	far away	(*fa-raway*)
carol	(*ca-rol*)	together again	(*togethe-ragain*)
lingering	(*linge-ring*)	forever and aye	(*fo-reve-rand aye*)
mystery	(*myste-ry*)	star above	(*sta-rabove*)

DOUBLE *r* IS SUNG AS ONE *r*

Only one *r* is pronounced, even when two appear consecutively. For example: *sorrow* (printed under the notes as *sor-row*) is sung as *so-row*. *Never rest* is sung as *neve-rest*.

r BEFORE SILENT LETTERS

Because silent letters appear only in spelling, and not in pronunciation, an *r* before a silent letter is governed by whatever follows the silent letter. When a sounded vowel follows, the *r* must be sung.

For example: *You are all*. The *e* in *are* is silent (*are*). Therefore, the *r* is followed by the sounded vowel *a* in *all,* and must be sung. The phrase is pronounced: *you ah-rall.*

Practice singing:

where am I	(*whe-ram I*)
you are all	(*you ah-rall*)
before us	(*befo-rus*)
for honor	(*fo-ronor*)

At this stage, you will find it helpful to make indicative marks on your musical material, crossing out every *r* that is to be omitted and underlining every *r* that is to be sounded. In a surprisingly short time, your ear will be accustomed to the sound of the correct use of *r*.

6. WHICH KIND OF *r* TO SING
BEFORE A VOWEL

We shall now consider which kind of *r* is sung, remembering that the only time *r* is sung at all is before a vowel.

The chart below offers a bird's eye view of the recommended procedures. It will be followed by a detailed explanation.

WHICH KIND OF *r* TO SING BEFORE A VOWEL

Use the flipped *r* in:
OPERA

One exception: American *r* in *tr* or *dr* combinations

Use the American *r* in:
SACRED MUSIC
ART SONGS

Three exceptions: Flipped *r*
1. Between vowels.
2. On your highest tones.
3. When *cr* or *gr* combinations occur in words that are
   a) dramatic or
   b) difficult to project

Use only the American *r* in:
ALL OTHER TYPES OF MUSIC
Popular Songs
"Semi-Classic" Ballads
Musical Comedy and
    Operetta
Folk Songs
Songs of American
    Locale
Juvenile Songs, when
    singer characterizes
    child

Two exceptions:
GILBERT AND SULLIVAN
BRITISH FOLK SONGS
(Both follow art-song
procedure)

r IN OPERA

Use the flipped *r*

The flipped *r* is, in its essence, more penetrating than the American *r*. Therefore, the flipped *r* is a necessity in opera, because you must have available every device for articulating above a large orchestra, placed between you and the audience. Over heavy accompaniments, singers are tempted to push their voices, with inevitable damage to vocal quality.

The best vehicles for the fullest projection of tone are the consonants. And because the flipped *r* has more propulsive power than the American *r*, the flipped *r* is the one to be used in works involving a strong instrumental complement.

In the following examples, *fl* under an *r* indicates a flipped *r;* a line through an *r* indicates that it is omitted:

I shall be you~r~ se~r~vant,

I shall be you~r~ princess,
         fl

I shall be you~r~ foreign bride . . .   (*The Medium;* Menotti)
        fl   *fl*

Come, dearest bride-to-be, now that I've found you
    fl   *fl*

I see ou~r~ family gathe~r~ed around you.
               fl

    I'll be so proud of them,
     fl

    The~r~e'll be a crowd of them.
       fl

Three little gi~r~ls and three little boys.
fl   *fl*

           (Donizetti's *Don Pasquale;* Phyllis Mead transl.)

EXCEPTION: USE THE AMERICAN *r* IN THE COMBINATIONS *tr* OR *dr*

Even in opera, use an American *r* in the combinations *tr* and *dr*, either within a word (*trust* or *dream*) or in immediately adjoining words (*last rose* or *sad recollection*). The consonants *t* and *d* are strong tongue consonants which propel the American *r* sufficiently clearly and which would cause the flipped *r* to sound trilled and overdone.

Examples:

truth	the light reveals
treasure	thou shalt reap
strange	hope must rise
entreat	do you not recall
distress	would fate release me
mistress	violent wrath
draw	glad rejoicing
dread	kneel and repent
drown	hope would rise
drink	love did remain
children	his hated rival
hundred	wide road

In the following illustrations, *Am* under an *r* indicates an American *r:*

May my wrongs create no trouble in thy breast.
    fl   *fl*   *Am*   *fl*

(Dido and Aeneas; Tate; Purcell)

Stop staring at me. You don't want to answer. You're trying to
   fl   *Am*
frighten me.   (*The Medium;* Menotti)
fl

They live on borrowed breath . . . No ship nor shore for him
                   fl   *fl*
who drowns at sea . . . Dreams are never true.
 Am   *Am*   *Am*

(The Consul; Menotti)

WHEN TO AVOID THE *tr* AND *dr* EXCEPTION

When *tr* or *dr* occurs on an extremely high note which causes the American *r* to be difficult to sing, avoid the exception and sing the flipped *r* as a necessary expedient. (On your very highest tones, the flipped *r* is easier than the American.) However, this expedient should be used only as a last resort; always try the American *r* first.

A NOTE ON *r* IN RECITATIVO SECCO

Recitativo secco, translated literally, is dry recitative. It is a term used in opera to designate the type of recitative that is accompanied only by an occasional chord from piano, harpsichord, or strings. It occurs frequently in the operas of Mozart and Rossini as well as others that take us up to the present day. This kind of recitative is intoned dialogue and should be pronounced like dialogue. (It will be discussed more fully on pp. 95-96.)

1. Use the flipped *r* between vowels only.
2. Use the American *r* otherwise.

OPERA IN TELEVISION OR RADIO STUDIOS

When singing opera in a television or radio studio, the flipped *r* is less necessary than in an opera house. Use the rules for art songs. Reason: The use of a microphone and electrically controlled balance of voice and orchestra reduces the need for extensive use of the flipped *r*.

r IN SACRED MUSIC AND ART SONGS

'Ve repeat the directions so that you will not be obliged to turn back to page 16.)

Use the American *r* with three exceptions.

IN THE EXCEPTIONS, USE THE FLIPPED *r*.

EXCEPTION 1. BETWEEN VOWELS (*spirit, for us*).

EXCEPTION 2. ON YOUR HIGHEST TONES.

EXCEPTION 3. WHEN *cr* OR *gr* COMBINATIONS OCCUR IN WORDS
THAT ARE

A) DRAMATIC (*cruel, grief*) OR

B) DIFFICULT TO PROJECT (*crag, grove*).

When the accompanying instruments are not situated between the singer and the audience, there is less need for the projecting power of the flipped *r*. In art songs and sacred music, including oratorio, the piano, organ, or, on occasion, orchestral players are not placed in the foreground, as they are in opera, and the singer need not "make himself heard across them." Thus, the American *r* is, in general, sufficient. There are, however, three important exceptions which are based on purely stylistic and vocal considerations.

EXCEPTION 1. USE A FLIPPED *r* BETWEEN VOWELS.

The texts of sacred music and art songs have an inherent dignity and literary quality that are best conveyed by use of the flipped *r* between vowels.

Examples of sacred music:

Let the spirit of this child return.
fl   *Am*

Oh, that I knew where I might find him, that I might even come
fl

before his presence . . . Who hath believed ouʀ repoʀt; to whom is
    Am   *fl*

the aʀm of the Loʀd revealed? Thus saith the Loʀd, the Redeemer
              Am   *fl*   *fl*

of Israel, and his Holy One, to him oppressed by tyrants.
 Am   *Am*   *fl*

                                        (*Elijah;* Mendelssohn)

That heʀ waʀfare is accomplished, that her iniquity is paʀdoned.
             fl   *fl*

Arise, shine, foʀ thy light is come.
 fl

Rejoice greatly, O daughter of Jerusalem . . . He is the righteous
Am   *Am*   *fl*   *fl*   *fl*

saviouʀ . . . The trumpet shall sound, and the dead shall be raised
                    Am   *fl*

incorruptible.   (*Messiah;* Handel)
 fl

Examples of art songs:

    The fountains mingle with the riveʀ —
                                fl

    And the riveʀs with the ocean,
               fl

    The winds of heaven mix for eveʀ
                                fl

    With a sweet emotion . . .

                          (*Love's Philosophy;* Shelley, Quilter)

    Bright is the ring of woʀds
    Am   [*fl*

        When the right man rings them,
             fl   *Am*

    Faiʀ the fall of songs

        When the singeʀ sings them.

    Still they aʀe carolled and said —
            fl

        On wings they aʀe carried —
               fl

    Afteʀ the singer is dead
            fl

        And the makeʀ buried.
               fl

    (*Songs of Travel;* R. L. Stevenson, R. Vaughan Williams)

EXCEPTION 2. USE A FLIPPED *r* ON YOUR HIGHEST TONES.

When an *r* that would normally be an American *r* occurs on one of your highest tones, the flipped *r* is easier to sing. Therefore, use the flipped *r* in the extreme upper register. This procedure has the virtue of clarity as well as ease. The American *r* becomes inaudible on a high tone and, in these conditions, the flipped *r* will not seem exaggerated.

Reminder: Never sing *r* before a consonant. If you ignore this rule on high tones, you will damage them severely.

EXCEPTION 3. USE THE FLIPPED *r* WHEN *cr* OR *gr* COMBINATIONS OCCUR IN WORDS THAT ARE EITHER DRAMATIC OR DIFFICULT TO PROJECT.

The initial consonants of the combinations *cr* and *gr* are formed at the back of the tongue, and the flipped *r* brings these sounds forward, supplying impact to words of dramatic significance and clarifying words that may otherwise not be readily understandable. The flipping of *r* in *cr* and *gr* combinations, however, should be specifically limited to such words.

Examples of dramatic words:

cruel	crumble	grief	grim
crush	cringe	grieve	growl
cry (in its emotional sense)		grave	groans

O blown, whirling leaf,
And the old *grief*,
        fl
And wind *crying* to me who am old and blind!
        fl
            (*The Lament of Ian the Proud;* MacLeod, Griffes)
I am slain by a fair *cruel* maid . . .
                fl
Where true lover never find my *grave*
    Am   *fl*
To weep there.   (*Come Away, Death;* Shakespeare, Quilter)

Examples of words difficult to project:

crag	grove
creed	growth
crude	grotto

In leafy arches twine the shady *groves* . . .
                                     fl
                    (*With Verdure Clad,* from *The Creation;* Haydn)
Deep in the sun-searched *growths* . . .
                                     fl
                    (*Silent Noon;* D. G. Rossetti, Vaughan Williams)
I had a bunch of cowslips,
I hid them in a *grot* . . .
                fl   (*The Buckle;* De la Mare, Bliss)
Do not use the flipped *r* in *cr* or *gr* words that are undramatic,
unemotional, or unmistakable, such as:

cradle	crimson	green	grace
cream	crown	grass	gray
cry (in the sense of say)		grant	grain
		greet	grape

And step into your dairy below,
                fl
And fetch me a bowl of *cream.*
                            Am
                    (*May Day Carol,* Eng. Folk Song, arr. Deems Taylor)
She bid me take life easy
As the *grass grows* on the weirs . . .
    Am Am
                    (*Down by the Sally Gardens;* Yeats, Trad.)
And sea horses stabled in *great green* caves . . .
                          Am   Am
                    (*Sea Shell;* Amy Lowell, Carl Engel)

When two dramatic *cr* or *gr* words are adjacent, flip the *r* in
only one of them, to avoid something both melodramatic and ludicrous. Choose the word that is more important.

For example:

craven creature	grim grief
fl *Am*	*Am* *fl*

We suggest that you continue to make indicative marks on your
musical material, this time writing *Am* under each American *r,* and
fl under each flipped *r*. As usual, draw a line through each *r* that is to
be omitted. Follow this practice for several weeks, consulting the
chart on page 16 frequently. Eventually, you will not find it necessary to refer to the book. Your ear will be trained to guide you.

r IN ALL OTHER TYPES OF MUSIC

Use only the American r.

POPULAR SONGS AND "SEMI-CLASSIC" BALLADS

MUSICAL COMEDY AND OPERETTA

FOLK SONGS

SONGS OF AMERICAN LOCALE

JUVENILE SONGS, IN WHICH THE SINGER
CHARACTERIZES THE CHILD

EXCEPTIONS:

GILBERT AND SULLIVAN

BRITISH FOLK SONGS

(Both Follow the Art-Song Procedure)

POPULAR SONGS AND "SEMI-CLASSIC" BALLADS

Popular songs are sung as they might be talked — with the American *r* exclusively. This is the only accepted style of pronunciation in this field of music, and it extends also to many ballads generally described as "semi-classic." The flipped *r* would be an intrusion and a mannerism, and the singer who committed it would be labelled "concerty."

Examples:

A cigarette that bears a lipstick's traces,
    Am   *Am*
An airline ticket to romantic places,
                    Am
And still my heart has wings:
These foolish things remind me of you.
                    Am

(*These Foolish Things;** Strachey, Link, and Marvell)

MUSICAL COMEDY AND OPERETTA

Tne popular song style prevails in present-day musical comedy productions, and only the American *r* is used. Some of the older operettas were composed somewhat in a grand opera manner, but even these, when revived, are treated in the same way as new musical plays.

Present-day theater orchestration and playing are subordinated for the sake of the words. The same practice prevails when the older operettas are revived in modern playhouses. The propulsive power of the flipped *r* is not required.

---

*Copyright 1935 by Bourne, Inc., New York, New York. Used by permission of the copyright owners.

It is a professional fact that in current musical comedy and operetta productions the flipped *r* is virtually taboo. Producers do not want it, and do not engage singers who insist on using it. Example:

It seems we stood and looked like this before.
We looked at each other in the same way then,
                    Am
I can't remember where or when.
        Am   *Am*
            (*Where or When,** from *Babes in Arms;* Hart, Rodgers)

Exception: Gilbert and Sullivan

The light operas of Gilbert and Sullivan require a British flavor. Sing these with the art song procedure in which the pronunciation of *r* is identical with that of the British. The American *r* that is also required in that procedure can be clearly heard because the orchestration of such productions provides an accompaniment that is sufficiently light. Example:

Take a pair of sparkling eyes,
        fl
Hidden, ever and anon,
        fl
In a merciful eclipse —
Do not heed their mild surprise —
                    Am
Having passed the Rubicon,
        fl
Take a pair of rosy lips . . .
        fl   Am
                (From *The Gondoliers;* Gilbert and Sullivan)

FOLK SONGS

In singing folk songs, use the American *r* only, to convey the spirit of folk music in all its simplicity.

Also, in singing translations of folk music from other lands, use the American *r* only, to preserve the folk quality of the original. Example:

Oh, give me a home, where the buffalo roam,
                            Am
Where the deer and the antelope play;
        Am

---

*Where or When, Copyright 1937 by Chappell & Co., Inc. Used by permission.

Whe~~re~~ never is hea~~r~~d a discouraging wo~~r~~d,
　　　Am　　　　　　　　*Am*
And the skies a~~re~~ not cloudy all day.
Home, home on the range, etc.　　　(*Home on the Range*)
　　　　　Am

Exception: British Folk Songs

British folk music should be sung with the art song procedure, because the colloquial speech of Great Britain bears a similarity to that pronunciation.

I know where I'm goin',
　　　fl
And I know who's goin' with me,
I know who I love
But the dea~~r~~ knows who I'll marry.　(*I know where I'm goin'*)
　　　　　　　　　　fl

SONGS OF AMERICAN LOCALE

Obviously a song that deals in familiar language with American locale, activities, personages, or history is sung with an American *r*. Example:

He was only nine
The year I died.
　　Am
I remembe~~r~~ still,
　Am
How ha~~r~~d he cried . . .
　　　　Am
And a prairie wind
　Am Am
To blow him down . . .
Did he lea~~r~~n to read?
　　　　Am
Did he get to town?
　　　　(*Nancy Hanks — Abraham Lincoln's Mother;** Rosemary
　　　　　　　　　　Benét, Katherine K. Davis)

JUVENILE SONGS, in which the singer characterizes a child.

When a singer is voicing the sentiments of a child, the American *r* should be used to avoid the effect of sophistication. The flipped *r* would transform the child into an infant singing grand opera. Do not misunderstand this to imply that "baby talk" is desirable.

---

*Lines from "Nancy Hanks" by Rosemary Benét in *A Book of Americans* published by Rinehart & Company, Inc. Copyright, 1933, by Rosemary and Stephen Vincent Benét.

Example:

See the big ship we're sailing on,
Me and Donald and John,
We're going to fill her with pirate gold,
                              Am
And diamonds and nickels in the hold.
Pirates make a dreadful fuss
  Am   *Am*
That'd frighten you, but they can't scare us . . .
      Am   *Am*

                    (*Sailor Men;* Herb Roth, Jacques Wolfe)

*   *

*

A SPECIAL NOTE ON *thr*

What has been said about singing *tr* with an American *r* does
not apply to *thr*, and the two sounds should not be confused. *thr*
may be sung with a flipped *r* whenever you wish — even in popular
music — because the flipped *r* seems to follow naturally after *th*.
To illustrate:

| through | thread | throne | three |
| thrill | threat | throng | throat |

*   *

*

We have studied the fundamentals involved in the singing —
and non-singing — of the *r* sound. Later on, we shall consider a
few additional situations in which *r* plays a part, but it cannot be
urged too strongly that this section be mastered first.

7. *y:* SOMETIMES A CONSONANT, SOMETIMES A VOWEL

y is sometimes a consonant and sometimes a vowel, as you will recall from the elementary school listing of the vowels as *"a, e, i, o, u, and sometimes y."* It is important to identify the exact function of *y* in any syllable so that you will sing correctly any *r* that may precede it.

1. *y* is a consonant at the beginning of a syllable. Therefore *r* before a syllable beginning with *y* is omitted.

Practice singing:

for you   after yuletide

her youth   another year

their yoke   they were yielding

Where *e'er you* walk, cool gales shall fan the glade.
    fl

(From *Semele;* Handel)

O Mistress mine, where *are you* roaming?
    Am   *fl*   *fl*

(Shakespeare, Quilter)

2. *y* is a vowel in the middle or at the end of a syllable. Therefore, an *r* before a *y* occurring in the middle or at the end of a syllable must be sounded. For example: *rhyme, very.*

Before practicing the singing of *r* before the vowel *y*, note the following comment on the pronunciation of final unstressed *y*.

PRONUNCIATION OF FINAL UNSTRESSED *y*

Final *y* when unstressed should have the sound of *i* as in *it*. The phonetic symbol for this sound is [ɪ], which looks like capital I, but is much smaller

This pronunciation is not only correct but also is necessary to express the musical grace of words with this ending. If you pronounce final unstressed *y* as *ee*, you destroy the essential lightness of the sound. Do not be deceived by approximate rhymes. When a word

27

ending in *y*, like *memory*, is rhymed with a word like *me* or *see*, do not feel obliged to sing *memoree*.

Even when final unstressed *y* is prolonged by the music, the [ɪ] sound can be and should be maintained. It is just as easy to sustain [ɪ] in the word *memory* as in the word *still*.

Final *y* when stressed (*cry*, *decry*) or when slightly stressed (*outcry*) is, of course, pronounced like the word *eye*. It is entirely unlike a *y* that has no stress whatever.

The words listed below illustrate *y* in the middle or at the end of a syllable. Practice singing them, first with an American *r*, then with a flipped *r*.

rhyme	memory	marry
rhythm	carry	sorry
very	bury	hurry
merry	berry	worry

Ev'ry valley shall be exalted, and *ev'ry* mountain and hill made
   Am   *Am*
low . . . And the *glory* of the Lord shone round about them . . .
                 fl   *Am*

                                         (*Messiah;* Handel)

HOW TO CONNECT WORDS WITH INITIAL *y*

When a word ending in a consonant is followed by a word beginning with *y*, connect the two words by sounding the final consonant of the first word as the beginning of the second word. For example:

rob you	(*ro-byou*)	beside you	(*besi-dyou*)
beg your grace	(*be-gyour*)	I love you	(*I lo-vyou*)
not young	(*no-tyoung*)	tell you	(*te-lyou*)

CAUTION

Special care must be taken with the following combinations which are frequently mispronounced:

(*dyou*) Sing *beside you* as *besi-dyou*, not as *besi-djou*.

(*tyou*) Sing *want you* as *wan-tyou*, not as *wan-tchou*.

(*syou*) Sing *miss you* as *mi-syou*, not as *mi-shou*.

(*zyou*) Sing *loves you* as *lov-zyou*, not as *lov-jou*. (French *j*)

(*tsyou*) Sing *lets you* as *le-tsyou*, not as *le-shou*.

For special illustrative purposes, we have used *you* for each of the examples above, but the same caution should be exercised with all other words beginning with *y*.

8. VOICELESS AND VOICED CONSONANTS

Consonants are of two kinds: voiceless and voiced. For practical purposes, we may consider a voiceless consonant as one that can be whispered, and a voiced consonant as one that cannot be whispered. A voiceless consonant (for example: *t, f, p*) requires an audible blowing of air (which is also called aspiration) but no vocalized sound. A voiced consonant (for example: *d, v, b*) requires vocalized sound instead of the blowing of air.

For each voiceless consonant (except *h*), there is a corresponding voiced consonant, and the same position of the speech organs (lips, tongue, etc.) is used for each of the two consonants in any pair. For example: *t* and *d, f* and *v, p* and *b*.

PAIRS OF VOICELESS AND VOICED CONSONANTS

Voiceless	Voiced
t	*d*
f	*v*
p	*b*
k	*g* (as in *go*)
th (as in *thin*)	*th* (as in *thine*)
s	*z*
sh	*s* (as in *measure*)
ch .... {	*j* / *g* (as in *George*)
wh	*w*
h	[no partner]

It is highly important that the voiceless and voiced consonants be not interchanged (*d* for *t, f* for *v, b* for *p,* etc.) because this would result in a change of meaning (*dime* for *time, fine* for *vine, bray* for *pray,* etc.).

In addition to the pairs of consonants given above, there are voiced consonants that do not have a corresponding voiceless sound.

29

Voiced Consonants with No Corresponding Voiceless Sound

r

y (as in *you*)

m

n

ng (as in *sing*)

l

Voiceless Consonants in Singing

Some singers have a needless fear that aspiration of the voiceless consonants will rob them of their breath support, and they are reluctant to aspirate these consonants sufficiently.

Do not hesitate to blow enough air. These consonants do not use up the breath needed for singing. The aspiration of a voiceless consonant requires only an infinitesimal quantity of breath. There should be no vast exhalation or heaving from deep down in the lungs. The air that is expelled is merely the residual air that is always present in the mouth, and should be expelled only from the mouth.

Try the following experiment. Exhale beyond the normal limits until the lungs feel empty. Then pronounce *t* with an audible puff of air. It can be done easily. There is still enough air in lungs and mouth to make this aspirate sound. Try the same experiment with *f, p, k, s, sh, ch,* and voiceless *th.* It can be done with all of them. In fact, a voiceless consonant at the end of a long, sustained phrase is most helpful. For if you find that you are growing short of breath, it is encouraging to know that you will nevertheless be able to articulate the voiceless final consonant, without allowing your audience to become aware of your predicament.

Consonants Should Not Be Imploded in Singing

In speaking, the voiceless consonants *t, p,* and *k* are sometimes imploded, an imploded consonant being one that causes a stop without an explosion of air. To illustrate, the consonants that can be imploded in speech are underlined in the following phrases: *What danger threatens? Stop barking. A quick glance.* In speech, this implosion is often justifiable, especially when the voiceless consonant is followed by its voiced partner.

However, in singing, which, in general, is slower than speech, imploded consonants are undesirable. They cause an unpleasing and unmusical stop to the flow of sound, and give an impression of carelessness. Sing slowly: *What danger threatens? Stop barking. A quick glance,* imploding the underlined consonants, and you will hear the vocal dead-end. Although deliberately imploded consonants are useful in one category of music which will be mentioned presently, implosion should be avoided as a general practice.

"BREAKING THE LINE"

Some singers are reluctant to pronounce a well-aspirated voiceless consonant for fear of "breaking the line." This misapprehension is one of those old wives' tales that has no basis for the intelligent artist. "The line" is broken whenever there is a gap in it; and the neglect or omission of a voiceless consonant leaves a meaningless vacuum in the flow of the music as well as of the words. Far from "breaking the line," clearly articulated consonants help not only to express the full values of the song but also to focus and project the singer's tones.

9. *t* AND *d*

t (voiceless) and *d* (voiced) constitute a pair of consonants articulated by means of contact between the tip of the tongue and the upper gum ridge.

In our daily speech, many of us are careless about pronouncing *t*. A slovenly *t* may not be fatal to social conversation, but it is so damaging tó good singing diction that, even when all the other consonants are well enunciated, a *t* that is sloppy, muffled, or inaudible gives an impression of generally poor articulation. When any *t* is indistinctly projected or when it is missing, the listener will have difficulty in understanding the words, either in an auditorium or through a loudspeaker.

ARTICULATION OF *t*

1. Use only the tip of the tongue.

   Do not flatten the tongue against the upper gum ridge, as in pronouncing *n*.

2. Place the tongue tip against the upper gum ridge at a point well above the tooth line.

   Do not allow the tongue tip to touch the teeth, or even that part of the gum which adjoins the teeth. The result would be the thick *t* called the dentalized *t*, which is unacceptable in English.

   NOTE: A flattened tongue or a tongue touching the teeth would bring about the muted *t* of some other languages. A singer must have diction that is correct for the language he is singing, and must not carry over into English a pronunciation that applies only to a different language.

3. As the tongue leaves the gum, blow a slight puff of air.

   A *t* pronounced with no explosion of air becomes a *d*. In careless speech, people often say such things as "ride a ledder" (*write a letter*), "he is bedder" (*he is better*), "nod ad all" (*not at all*). This is absolutely unacceptable in singing. Every *t* must be a *t*.

32

The substitution of *d* for *t* is not only undesirable but often misleading. In many cases, it changes completely the meaning of a word.

Examples:

I am *wading* for you . . . (*waiting*)

At the *ladder* day . . . (*latter*) (*Messiah*)

Now sleeps the crimson *pedal* . . . (*petal*)

(Tennyson, Quilter)

They were *dripping* o'er the lawn . . . (*tripping*)

4. Move the tongue quickly.

Do not raise the tongue slowly to the gum. It would inadvertently give the effect of an *r*. For example: *haht* pronounced with a slow-moving tongue would sound like *heart* with an American *r*.

Do not allow the tongue to linger at the gum ridge while the *t* is being aspirated, for the result would be *ts*. This is done intentionally when pronouncing a word containing *ts,* such as *cats* or *cat's,* but must be avoided when singing *cat*. The action of the tongue must be quick as it leaves the gum.

DO NOT OMIT FINAL *t*

Final *t* may not be omitted. In careless speech, it is frequently neglected. We hear people say, "I mus' go home," "I dunno," "my coa' and ha'," "I'd rather nah," "the las' guess" (for *the last guest*).

In singing, such inaccuracies are inexcusable.

Now review the directions for the articulation of *t* and practice in a staccato manner:

. . . . .
t t t t t

Then practice singing the following (observe that double *t* is pronounced as one *t* and that *-ed* after a voiceless consonant is pronounced as *t*):

tip-top	waiting	put	hunt	felt	laughed
ten-times	letter	not	mountain	halt	talked
two-tones	better	fate	fountain	melt	worked
tiny-town	bitter	wait	winter	guilt	hoped
twice-told	pretty	mate	sent	wilt	blessed
take-two	thirty	right	plant	shalt	vanished
tin-trays	forty	sweet	twenty	built	watched
tree-trunk	writing	thought	seventy	dwelt	wept

t IS SOMETIMES A SILENT LETTER

The admonition never to omit a *t* does not apply, of course, to those words in which *t* is a silent letter. These words should be sung just as they are spoken. They include the following:

often,* soften, Christmas, chestnut
Words ending in *-sten* (such as *listen, glisten, fasten*)
Words ending in *-stle* (such as *thistle, castle, rustle*)
Words taken over from French (such as *ballet, bouquet, début, depot*)

SPECIAL NOTE ON *oft* AND *soft*

The fact that *t* is a silent letter in the words *often* and *soften* should not mislead the singer into concluding that it may be omitted in the words listed herewith.

The *t* must be sounded in:

oft	(do not sing *off*)
soft	(do not sing *soff*)
softer	(not *soffer*)
softest	(not *soffest*)
softly	(not *soffly*)
softness	(not *soffness*)

Practice singing:
Oft the tears are flowing,
Oft they flow from my mem'ry's treasure.
            (*Songs My Mother Taught Me;* MacFarren, Dvořák)
O so white, O so *soft*, O so sweet is she!
        (*Have You Seen But A White Lily Grow;* Ben Jonson)
Oh, men from the fields! Come gently within. Tread *softly,*
    softly . . .   (*Cradle Song;* Padraic Colum, Arnold Bax)

HOW TO CONNECT *t*
t BEFORE A VOWEL

When *t* is followed by a syllable or word beginning with a vowel, use the *t* as a connecting link, sounding it as the beginning of the next syllable or word. The *t* is sung in this direction (➤).

Remember that the vowel before the *t* must be sustained until the *t* is sounded.

---

*The pronunciation of *often* with a sounded *t* is accepted, but the omission of *t* is preferred.

Practice singing:

waiting	(*wai-ting*)	grant us	(*gran-tus*)
letter	(*le-ter*)	so sweet is she	(*swee-tis*)
water	(*wa-ter*)	not alone	(*no-talone*)
mountain	(*moun-tain*)	rest in peace	(*res-tin*)

It is enough (*i-tis*) . . . And they seek my life to take it away (*i-taway*).   (*Elijah;* Mendelssohn)

t BEFORE A CONSONANT

When *t* is followed by a consonant (as in *greatly* or *might be*), it must be sounded. In acceptable speech, it is often stopped without aspirating (imploded), but in singing, this is not permissible, since singing is more sustained than speech, and an imploded *t* would sound like a *t* carelessly omitted.

Hold the vowel that precedes the *t* as long as possible, sounding the *t* immediately before the next consonant, at the last split second. There should be an explosion of air between the *t* and the next consonant, but no vowel sound. The *t* and its succeeding consonant should be as close together as a grace note and its succeeding note with the stress on the second consonant.

Practice, with a well-aspirated *t*, but with no intervening vowel sound:

tB, tB	might be (*migh - - - tbe*)
tD, tD	sweet dream (*swee - - - tdream*)
tF, tF	set free (*se - - - tfree*)
tG, tG	do not go (*do no - - - tgo*)
tJ, tJ	great joy (*grea - - - tjoy*)
tK, tK	thou art kind (*thou ah - - - tkind*)
tL, tL	greatly (*grea - - - tly*)
tM, tM	await me (*awai - - - tme*)
tN, tN	let none (*le - - - tnone*)
tP, tP	night prayer (*nigh - - - tprayer*)
tTh, tTh	wilt thou (*wil - - - tthou*)
tV, tV	bright vision (*brigh - - - tvision*)

t BEFORE A PAUSE

When final *t* occurs before a pause, there must be a clear aspiration of the consonant, but no additional vowel sound.
Practice singing:

- - - in the night.   — as he wept —
- - - accept my fate.   - - - whom I love best.

FINAL *t* FOLLOWED BY A WORD BEGINNING WITH *t*

When final *t* is followed by a word beginning with *t*, the following considerations determine whether one *t* or both should be heard:
1. The slowness or rapidity of the tempo.
2. The formality or informality of the composition.
3. The importance of each of the two words.

For example:

Great triumph
(Slow tempo; sacred music, formal in style; each word important.)
Pronounce both *t*'s.

Great triumph
(Very quick tempo; any type of music, formal or informal.)
Pronounce only one *t*.

Great time (as sung in a popular song)
(Slow tempo, informal music.)
Implode the first *t;* explode the second.

At times
I went to see
(Any tempo. Any type of music. The prepositions *at* and *to* are unimportant.)
Pronounce only one *t* (the second).

Some words are combined so frequently as to give the feeling of one word (*night time*). Here, even in slow tempo and in formal music, the second *t* is sufficient.

FURTHER EXAMPLES OF *t*

O rest‿in the Lord; wai*t* patien*t*ly for Him . . . Commi*t* thy way un*t*o Him, and *t*rust‿in Him, and fre*t* no*t* thyself because of evil doers.   (*Elijah;* Mendelssohn)

Do no*t* go, my love,
Withou*t*‿asking my leave.
I have watche*d*‿all nigh*t*,   (*watch't*)
And now my eyes are heavy with sleep;
I fear les*t*‿I lose you when I am sleeping.
I star*t*‿up and *s*tretch my hands to *t*ouch you.
I ask myself, Is i*t*‿a dream?
Could I bu*t*‿en*t*angle your fee*t*‿with my hear*t*
And hold them fas*t* *t*o my breast!
                         (*Do Not Go, My Love;* Tagore, Hageman)

FINAL SYLLABLES SUCH AS -*tle* AND -*ten*

We all know that in speaking, final syllables such as -*tle* (*little*) and -*ten* (*kitten*) may be pronounced with no vowel sound between the *t* and *l*, or *t* and *n*. But in singing, it is imperative that there be a vowel sound between the two consonants because a syllable cannot be sung without a vowel sound. The *t* is aspirated at the tip of the tongue, in the usual procedure of singing this consonant, and the vowel to be sung is the neutral vowel. (For description of the neutral vowel, see Chapter 42.)

Practice singing (note that double *t* is sung as one *t*):

little (*li-tel*)	kitten (*ki-ten*)
battle (*ba-tel*)	forgotten (*forgo-ten*)

A NOTE ON *t* IN POPULAR SONGS AND DIALECTS

Most popular songs are extremely colloquial in text, and should, of course, be sung in a suitably familiar style. With lyrics of this character as well as in dialect songs, a free treatment of *t* usually is desirable. In such cases, too, the directions given for singing -*tle* and -*ten* syllables may be disregarded.

STS

Some singers encounter difficulty in pronouncing *rests, hosts, beasts,* etc. They sing *rests* as *ress* or *rets* or *retst,* becoming more and more tongue-twisted as they struggle. They will find it simple to think of the word as divided in this way: *res-ts.* The *ts* is the final sound in *puts, hits,* etc. No word generally used in English begins with this sound except the name of the tropical insect, the *tsetse.*

Practice as follows:

puts, hits, hats

tsetse, tsetse

ts, ts, ts, ts (without a subsequent vowel)

res - - - - ts (with two separate motions of the tongue: first to sound the *s;* then after a pause, to sound the *ts*)

Gradually shorten the pause between the *s* and *ts* (*res - - - ts, res - - ts*) until the two sounds are close together (*res - ts*).

More practice words:

hosts	lasts	hastes
ghosts	casts	wastes
beasts	mists	guests
feasts	twists	texts (*teks-ts*)

FINAL *t* FOLLOWED BY *s*

When final *t* is followed by a word beginning with *s*, it is helpful toward a good legato to sing the *t* as the start of the second word, using the *ts* sound mentioned above.

Practice singing:

secret sorrow	(*secre-tsorrow*)
great soul	(*grea-tsoul*)
night song	(*nigh-tsong*)

This principle is even more helpful when final *-st* is followed by a word beginning with *s*. Sing this combination as *s-ts*.

Practice singing:

lost souls	(*los-tsouls*)
first song	(*firs-tsong*)

. . . To die with thee again in sweetest sympathy. (*sweetes-tsympathy*)

(*Come Again;* Dowland)

d

d is the voiced consonant corresponding to voiceless *t*.

ARTICULATION OF *d*

1. Use only the tip of the tongue.

   Do not flatten the tongue against the upper gum ridge, as in pronouncing *n*.

2. Place the tongue tip against the upper gum ridge at a point well above the tooth line.

   Do not allow the tongue tip to touch the teeth, or even that part of the gum which adjoins the teeth. The result would be the thick *d* called the dentalized *d*, which is unacceptable in English.

3. As the tongue leaves the gum ridge, add voice.

   There should be no explosion of air, because this would bring about a *t*.

Practice singing:

day	dark	dream	daughter
die	done	danger	dazzle
do	dome	dagger	doom

THE FINAL SYLLABLES -*dle* AND -*den*

In speaking, the final syllables -*dle* (*riddle*) and -*den* (*sudden*) are pronounced with no vowel sound between the *d* and *l*, or *d* and *n*. But in singing, there must be a vowel sound between the two consonants because a syllable cannot be sung without a vowel sound. The vowel of these syllables is the neutral vowel as in the case of -*tle* and -*ten*.

Practice singing (note that double *d* is sung as one *d*):

riddle (*ri-del*)   sudden (*su-den*)

idle (*i-del*)   hidden (*hi-den*)

How to Connect *d*

d BEFORE A VOWEL

When a syllable or word ending in *d* is followed by a syllable or word beginning with a vowel, use the *d* as a connecting link, sounding it as the beginning of the next syllable. The *d* moves in this direction (➤).

Practice singing:

sending (*sen-ding*)   send it (*sen-dit*)

wider (*wi-der*)   beside us (*besi-dus*)

faded (*fa-ded*)   ride away (*ri-daway*)

radiance (*ra-diance*)   confide in (*confi-din*)

d BEFORE A CONSONANT AND BEFORE A PAUSE

There is a special treatment for *d* before a consonant and before a pause, and because this is the same as for *b* and "hard" *g*, the connecting of these three consonants will be discussed simultaneously in Chapter 17.

10. LIP CONSONANTS

One of the most important principles of good diction and good singing is relaxation of the lips in the projection of the lip consonants: *p* and *b, f* and *v*, and *m*.

Relaxed lips bring about clear consonants that carry. Relaxed lips also result in relaxed throat muscles that bring about free tones. Tight lips cause inaudible consonants, constricted throat muscles, and pinched tones. Many singers struggle and strain to articulate the lip consonants with tight lips; all that they achieve from this painful technique is a kind of squeaking and squawking sound through which no words are intelligible. Actors who must go through eight performances a week know that their speaking voices would fail them unless the lips were relaxed. It is essential for them to maintain the lip relaxation principle. It is equally essential for singers.

Let us demonstrate the principle by first going about it in the wrong way. Rest the palm of your hand against your throat while you sing the following words with tense, tight lips:

beauty	fury	memory
peace	vision	

What happens? Feel how the muscles of your neck stand out. Listen to the ugly, laborious tones. Note that your words are far from clear.

Now, with very relaxed, rubber-like lips, sing the same words, still touching the palm of the hand to the throat. What happens? The muscles of your neck are in repose, your voice sounds free, and your consonants are more audible than before. They will be even more audible when you have learned the special technique for articulating each of the five lip consonants, as described in the following chapters.

11. LIP CONSONANTS:
p AND *b*

p (voiceless) and *b* (voiced) constitute a pair of consonants articulated by means of the lips. In studying these consonants, we shall, for practical purposes, begin with the second member of the pair, *b*.

As a preliminary exercise, pout the lips; then with the fingertips, move the lips from side to side and up and down until they are completely relaxed. This establishes the basic relaxation required.

ARTICULATION OF *b*

1. Protrude the lips in the form of a pout, touching them together lightly.

Do not make a thin line of the lips.

2. Keeping the lips very relaxed, bounce them up and down against each other like soft rubber cushions, saying *buh-buh-buh-buh-buh*.

Do not press the lips together tightly.

3. Use only the inner surface of the lips.

Now say, very slowly, with the inner surfaces of the lips bouncing against each other:

bubble-babble-bauble

The ba-by bounced the big brown ball.

Repeat the sentence, this time singing it, on any notes.

Practice singing:

bubble	beauty	bitter
babble	burning	better
bauble	bounty	abide
rabble	broken	abounding
trouble	breeze	abyss

mb

When one syllable ends in *m,* and the next begins with *b* (as in *slumber*), be sure to bounce the lips so that the *b* can be heard.

slumber   September   mumble   tremble

41

| number | November | rumble | resemble |
| remember | December | crumble | thimble |

SILENT *b*

Do not forget that *b* is silent in words ending in *mb*.
For example:

comb	lamb	thumb
climb	tomb	dumb
crumb		plumb

SPECIAL CAUTIONS

Do not substitute *m* for *b*, singing *mut* for *but*, *mad* for *bad*, *mall* for *ball*, *mannish* for *banish*. This substitution is a frequent fault against which singers must guard. The differentiation between *m* and *b* is insured by bouncing the lips when sounding *b*.

Another careless habit is that of sounding a superfluous *m* before an initial *b* (*mbut* for *but*, *mbeauty* for *beauty*) at the beginning of a phrase. This happens because singers sometimes sound the pitch ahead of the word. Do not let your audience hear you fumbling — or mumbling — for the correct note. Learn to be aware of the pitch inwardly ("have it in your ear," as the saying is), and start the phrase cleanly with the consonant.

Practice singing, taking care to differentiate:

mut, but	mare, bear	mind, bind
mad, bad	more, bore	mound, bound
mall, ball	morn, born	mold, bold

Examples of *b* in song texts:

My mother *b*ids me *b*ind my hair
With *b*ands of rosy hue,
Tie up my sleeves with ri*b*ands rare
And lace my *b*odice *b*lue.

(*My Mother Bids Me Bind My Hair;* Haydn)

Go 'way from my window,
Go 'way from my door,
Go 'way, 'way, 'way from my *b*edside
And *b*other me no more.
I'll go tell all my *b*rothers,
Tell all my sisters too,
That the reason why my heart is *b*roke
Is on account of you . . .

Remem*b*er, dear, that you're the one
I really did love *b*est.
(Go 'Way from My Window; John Jacob Niles)

I *b*een a-ram*b*ling all this night,
And some time of this day,
And now returning *b*ack again,
I *b*rought you a *b*ranch of May . . .
'Tis nothing *b*ut a sprout, *b*ut well *b*udded out . . .
(May Day Carol; arr. Deems Taylor)

EXPRESSIVENESS

Do not hesitate to sound a good *b* even in words of tenderness such as *baby, lullaby,* etc. Some singers fancy that they increase expressiveness by a muffling of the *b* in gentle sentiments, but this practice eliminates the expressiveness along with the *b*.
Practice singing with a soft voice, but with a distinctly intelligible *b:*

Sleep, my pretty one, close to mother,
*B*ye o' *b*aby *b*ye!
Mother tells her *b*edtime stories,
Croons her lulla*b*y!
(Slumber Song; transl. Baum, Gretchaninow)

How to Connect *b*

b BEFORE A VOWEL

When *b* is followed by a syllable or word beginning with a vowel, use it as a connecting link, sounding it as the beginning of the next syllable or word, moving in this direction (→). The vowel sound of course does not change.

For example (note that double *b* is sung as one *b*):

robber	(*ro-ber*)	web of dreams	(*we-bof dreams*)
sobbing	(*so-bing*)	rob us	(*ro-bus*)
table	(*ta-bel*)	sob in secret	(*so-bin secret*)

b BEFORE A CONSONANT AND BEFORE A PAUSE

When *b* occurs before a consonant or before a pause, it requires special treatment. This will be discussed in Chapter 17.

p

p is the voiceless consonant corresponding to *b,* which is voiced.

ARTICULATION OF *p*

1. Protrude the lips in the form of a pout, touching them together lightly.

Do not make a thin line of the lips.

2. Keeping the lips very relaxed, blow out a narrow stream of air, directing it against the center of the upper lip, causing the lips to open.

Do not press the lips together tightly.

To test whether you are aspirating the *p* sufficiently, hold a piece of paper in front of the mouth for a moment, and pronounce a *p*, blowing with just sufficient air to move the corner of the paper. This quantity of air is necessary for the clear articulation of this consonant.

3. Use only the inner surface of the lips.

Do not "turn the lips outside in," as an old saying has it.

4. It is important to realize that in pronouncing *p*, no vocal tone is added as for *b*.

Practice singing:

pin point	sleep	drop	clasp (not *class*)
puppet	weep	trap	grasp (not *grass*)
poppy	deep	up	hope (not *hoe*)
poor pauper	keep	cup	lamp (not *lamb*)
poisoned pool	creep	trip	help (not *hel'*)

More examples:

A *plump* and *p*leasing *p*erson (*H.M.S. Pinafore;* Gilbert and
Sullivan)

I heard a *p*iper *p*iping the blue hills among
And never heard I so *p*laintive a song.
It seemed but a *p*art of the hills melancholy.
No *p*iper *p*iping there could ever be jolly.
And still the *p*iper *p*iped the blue hills among;
And all the birds were quiet to listen to his song.

(*I Heard a Piper Piping;* Campbell, Bax)

DIFFERENTIATE BETWEEN *b* AND *p*

Many singers fail to differentiate between *b* and *p*. This negligence automatically changes the words that are to be sung and may result in the expression of alarming sentiments, not intended by the poet.

Practice singing the paired words below, taking care to differentiate between them:

Do not sing

bride - pride	"I swallow my *bride*."
blight - plight	"My sorry *blight*."
breach - preach	"*Breach* not me your musty rules."
	(misquotation of *Air* from *Comus;* Milton, Arne)
bath - path	"The very *bath* by which I wander . . ."
	(misquotation of *Pilgrim's Song;* transl. England, Tchaikovsky)
bleed - plead	"Your *bleeding* eyes."
bray - pray	"I hear her *braying*."

EXPRESSIVENESS

The stream of air that is blown in singing *p* provides not only clarity, but also expressiveness. For example, the word *pain* is more poignant when its initial consonant is well aspirated.

With this in mind, practice singing:

pain	pure	plea
pity	peace	appeal
pining	passion	implore

The *Prince* of *peace* . . . and He shall speak *peace* . . .

(*Messiah;* Handel)

In deadly *pain* and endless misery.   (*Come Again;* Dowland)

DO NOT IMPLODE *p*

In speaking, *p* followed by *t* (as in *rapture*) is often imploded. That is, the *p* is stopped but not exploded. In singing, this implosion is undesirable. The flow of tone seems much less to be impeded by a consonant that is audible than by a stop for one that is not heard. It is not only for this reason but also because the slower tempo of singing makes the loss of this consonant more apparent than in speaking, that the *p* should be aspirated in all the words below.

Practice singing with an aspirate *p* (note that double *p* is sung as one *p*):

rapture	leaped	temptation
scripture	wept	except
heaped	slept	swept
stopped	empty	capture (not *catcher*)
dropped	attempt	rapt (not *rat*)

The wind has drop*p*ed and the sky's deranged.
Summer has stop*p*ed.
(Ah, Love But a Day; Protheroe, Beach)

Rose leaves, when the rose is dead
Are hea*p*'d for the beloved's bed . . .
(Music When Soft Voices Die; Shelley, Quilter)

A NOTE ON THE WORD *spell*

The word *spell*, in its poetic sense, meaning magic or enchant-ment, is often heard to emerge, in song, as *smell*. To correct this untoward transformation, first repeat "pell" several times, with a well aspirated *p*. Then say *s* and stop; then say "pell." Repeat *s* - - (stop) - - *pell* several times, gradually shortening the stop between *s* and *pell* until the two sounds are almost together. They can never really be joined, because the *s* would cause the *p* to resemble *b*, which may, under these circumstances, sound too strongly like *m*.

HOW TO CONNECT *p*

p BEFORE A VOWEL

When *p* is followed by a syllable or word beginning with a vowel, use it as a connecting link, sounding it as the start of the next syllable or word. It moves in this direction (➤).
Practice singing:

sleeping	(*slee-ping*)	sleep in peace	(*slee-pin*)
clasping	(*clas-ping*)	cup of cheer	(*cu-puv*)
happy	(*ha-py*)	rap on the door	(*ra-pon*)
rapid	(*ra-pid*)	slip into the forest	(*sli-pinto*)
vapor	(*va-por*)	hope and light	(*ho-pand*)

p BEFORE A CONSONANT

When *p* is followed by a consonant, hold the vowel preceding the *p* as long as possible, pronouncing the *p* immediately before the next consonant. The *p* and its following consonant should be as close together as a grace note and its succeeding note. There should be an explosion of air between the *p* and the next consonant, but no vowel sound.

Practice, with a well-aspirated *p* but no intervening vowel sound:

pB, pB	deep bitterness	(*dee-pbitterness*)
pD, pD	drop down	(*dro-pdown*)
pF, pF	leap forth	(*lea-pforth*)

pG, pG	sharp gaze	(*shah-pgaze*)
pK, pK	hope kindles	(*ho-pkindles*)
pM, pM	keep me safe	(*kee-pme safe*)
pN, pN	weep not	(*wee-pnot*)
pQ, pQ	sleep quietly	(*slee-pquietly*)
pT, pT	stop to listen	(*sto-pto*)
pTh, pTh	help them	(*hel-pthem*)
pV, pV	the cup vanished	(*cu-pvanished*)

The final syllable -*ple* must have a neutral vowel between the *p* and *l*, when sung, because there can be no syllable in singing without a vowel sound. The neutral vowel is discussed in Chapter 42. Examples:

people	ripple
apple	simple
steeple	trample

FINAL *p* BEFORE INITIAL *p*

When a word ending in *p* is followed by a word beginning with *p*, use the same procedure as for *t*. In slow, dignified music, pronounce both. In moderate tempi, pronounce both only if the words are of equal importance and must be detached for the sake of clarity. Otherwise, one *p* is sufficient.

Examples:
deep prayer
keep peace
Your hel*p* proud Caesar craves. (*Hear Me, Ye Winds and Waves,*
from *Scipio;* Handel)

Further Examples of *p:*
I attem*p*t from love's sickness to fly in vain
Since I am myself my own fever and *p*ain.
No more, now, fond heart, with *p*ride should we swell,
Thou canst not raise forces enough to rebel.
For love has more *p*ow'r and less mercy than fate
To make us seek ruin, and love those that hate.
(*I Attempt from Love's Sickness to Fly,* from *The Indian
Queen;* Howard, Purcell)

Her hair is long, her eyes are dee*p*
And sapphire like the waves;
She has no grief to make her wee*p*,
And goldfish are her slaves. (*Corals;* Akins, Treharne)

12. LIP CONSONANTS:
f AND *v*

f (voiceless) and *v* (voiced) constitute a pair of consonants articulated by means of the lower lip and upper teeth.

As a preliminary exercise, place a fingertip between lower lip and chin and, by means of the fingertip, move your lower lip sideways and up and down until it is completely relaxed. Then proceed.

ARTICULATION OF *f*

1. Place the lower lip outside of and over the upper teeth. Raise the upper lip just enough so that it will not interfere.

> Do not place the lower lip inside of the upper teeth.
> Raise the lower lip sufficiently for the upper teeth to make contact well down inside of it.

2. Keep the lower lip very relaxed.

> Do not tense or tighten it.

3. Touch the inside of the lower lip against the edges of the upper teeth very lightly.

> Do not bite into your lip. If the lower lip is bitten, or tightly pressed against the teeth, the air is stopped, and the consonant cannot be heard.

4. Blow a puff or stream of air sufficient to be audible.

> There should be no vocalized sound.

There are many dramatic words that begin or end in *f*, and if they are not well aspirated with a relaxed lower lip, their expressiveness is lost.

Practice singing:

fury	fame	free	grief	life
fear	fortune	fond	strife	wife
fire	friend	find	knife	laugh
flame	farewell	first	brief	leaf
fate	father	few	enough	nymph

And he shall *f*eed his *f*lock . . . For he is like a re*f*iner's *f*ire . . .

(*Messiah;* Handel)

*F*ull *f*athom *f*ive thy *f*ather lies . . .

(Shakespeare; Robert Johnson)

I have desired to go
Where springs not *f*ail,
To *f*ields where *f*lies no sharp and sided hail
And a *f*ew lilies blow. (*A Nun Takes the Veil;* Hopkins, Barber)

How to Connect *f*

f before a vowel

When *f* is followed by a syllable or word beginning with a vowel use the *f* as a connecting link, sounding it as the beginning of the next syllable or word. The *f* moves in this direction (➤). The vowel sound of course does not change.

Practice singing (note that double *f* is pronounced as one *f*):

laughing	(*la-fing*)	if it is here	(*i-fi-tis*)
suffer	(*su-fer*)	life and death	(*li-fand*)
coffin	(*co-fin*)	chief among them	(*chie-famong*)

f before a consonant

When *f* is followed by a consonant, hold the vowel preceding the *f* as long as possible and pronounce the *f* immediately before the next consonant. There should be a blowing of air between the *f* and the next consonant, but no vowel sound. The *f* and its following consonant should be as close together as a grace note and its succeeding note.

Practice:

strife-borne	(*stri - - fborne*)	if not	(*i - - fnot*)
grief dwells	(*grie - - fdwells*)	life passes by	(*li - - - fpasses*)
belief grows	(*belie - - fgrows*)	lift	(*li - - ft*)
safe journey	(*sa - - fjourney*)	laughter	(*la - - fter*)
brief moment	(*brie - - fmoment*)	rough shore	(*rou - - fshore*)
	griefs (*grie - - fs*, NOT *grease*)		

f followed by *f* or *v*

When a word ending in *f* is followed by a word beginning with *f* or *v*, connect the two words as if they were one longer word. In the first case, sing a long, continuous *f*.

For example:

if friends meet	(*iffriends meet*)
grief finds us	(*grieffinds us*)
chief virtue	(*chieffvirtue*)
gruff voice	(*gruffvoice*)

f BEFORE A PAUSE

When *f* occurs before a pause, blow a stream of air of more than usual duration, allowing the lower lip to remain in contact with the upper teeth, all the while.

Do not pull the lower lip away from the teeth abruptly.

Do not allow any vowel sound to follow the *f*.

Practice singing:

. . . all my life.

My heart is full of grief.

. . . the end of our strife.

FURTHER EXAMPLES OF *f*

*F*low, my tears, *f*all from your springs.

Exiled *f*orever let me mourn;

Where night's black bird her sad in*f*amy sings

There let me live *f*orlorn.

No nights are dark enou*gh* ⌣ *f*or those

That in despair their lost *f*ortunes deplore

Light doth but shame disclose.

> (*Flow, My Tears;* Dowland)

Give to me the li*fe* ⌣ I love, . . .

There's the li*fe* ⌣ for a man like me,

There's the li*fe* ⌣ *f*orever . . .

Or let autumn *f*all on me

Where a*f*ield I linger,

Silencing the bird on tree,

Biting the blue *f*inger.

White as meal the *f*rosty *f*ield

Warm the *f*ireside haven . . .

> (*The Vagabond,* from *Songs of Travel;* R. L. Stevenson, Vaughan Williams)

v

v is the voiced partner of *f*, in the pair *f* and *v*. The position of lower lip and upper teeth is the same for these two consonants, but *f* is voiceless and *v* is voiced.

ARTICULATION OF *v*

There are four directions. For the first three, see page 48. The fourth direction is entirely unlike the fourth direction for articulation of *f*.

4. Instead of blowing air, as for *f*, add vocal tone sufficient to give the *v* a vibrant, buzzing sound.

Because the formation of lips and teeth is an individual physical feature in everyone's facial structure, each singer must locate the most efficient point of contact between the edges of his upper front teeth and his lower lip. Experiment until you find the exact spot inside your lower lip where its contact with the edges of the upper front teeth makes the most vibrant, buzzing sound.

You will know when the right point of contact is found because there will be a tickling sensation in your lower lip when you are singing the *v* effectively. This tickling sensation is caused by the vibration of the *v*, and this vibration helps to produce a rich, velvety sound. A relaxed, buzzing, vibrating *v* accomplishes three results: clarity, vocal beauty, and great expressiveness.

DIRECTIONS FOR PRACTICE

First, using your speaking voice, sound a *v* that buzzes for the duration of five or six slow counts.

When you have succeeded in making the spoken *v* buzz sufficiently, use your singing voice to sound a *v* that buzzes, for another five or six slow counts.

When this sung *v* buzzes sufficiently, sing it in the following words:

voice	velvet
vision	vain
virtue	vile
valor	villain

More I would, but death invades me. (*Dido and Aeneas;* Tate, Purcell)

With *v*erdure clad, the fields appear . . . (*The Creation;* Haydn)

We shall walk in *v*elvet shoes . . . (*Velvet Shoes;* Wylie, Thompson)

How to Connect *v*

v differs in two respects from the consonants we have studied so far:

1. It is not always connected in a forward direction.
2. One *v* is sung as though it were double *v*.

v BETWEEN VOWELS ON THE SAME PITCH

When *v* occurs between two vowels on the same pitch, start the *v* early, using part of the time value of the vowel that comes before it, in this direction (**←**).

For example:

divine	(*divv-ine*)	thy voice	(*thyvv-oice*)
devotion	(*devv-otion*)	a vision	(*avv-ision*)
revenge	(*revv-enge*)	so vain	(*sovv-ain*)

v BETWEEN VOWELS ON TWO DIFFERENT PITCHES

Here is a vital principle whose mastery will be a great asset in expressive singing.

When *v* occurs between two vowels that are on different pitches, sing the *v* on the pitch of the lower of the two notes, since the lower pitch will give more resonance to the *v*. Thus, *v* is sung in either direction (**←** or **→**), depending on the rise or fall of the musical interval.

When the first note is on the lower pitch, start the *v* early, sounding it as part of the first syllable, in this direction (**←**).
To illustrate:

divv - ine

When the second note is on the lower pitch, the *v* starts the second syllable, in this direction (**→**).
To illustrate:

di - vvine

CAUTION

Do not sing the *v* on both pitches. This effort would cause a disagreeable scoop. The *v* must be sung on one pitch only.

REMINDER ABOUT *r* BEFORE A CONSONANT

Remember that *r* before a consonant is omitted. Therefore, in words like *fervent* (*fe̶rvent*) and phrases like *her voice* (*he̶r voice*) the *v* occurs between vowels.

SPECIAL NOTE ON *I love you*

I love you, a phrase that appears more frequently than perhaps any other in the singer's vocabulary, deserves a special paragraph. Although initial *y* is a consonant, *v* followed by initial *y* is treated like *v* followed by a vowel. Therefore, the *v* in *I love you* is sung as a *v* between vowels. (*I lovyou* is sung like *I loview*.)

Practice each of the following words and phrases twice, first with a rising and then a falling interval:

divine	forever	save us	
devotion	never	a vision	
beloved	prevail	her voice	I love you
Saviour	revenge	so vain	
reveal	evil	their vanity	

Examples from vocal literature:

For unto you is born this day, in the city of David, a Saviour . . .
(Messiah; Handel)

Delightful to the ra*v*ish'd sense . . .   (*The Creation;* Haydn)

My son re*v*i*v*eth . . . To whom is the arm of the Lord re*v*ealed . . .
(Elijah; Mendelssohn)

I see your *v*ision nearing . . .
With your beloved name . . .
(In the Silence of Night; transl. Harris, Jr. and Deems Tay-
lor, Rachmaninoff)

Under *v*eils of white lace.   (*Velvet Shoes;* Wylie,* Thompson)

My lo*v*e and I did meet . . .

She bid me take lo*v*e easy . . . (*Down by the Sally Gardens;*
Yeats, Trad.)

v BEFORE A CONSONANT

When *v* is followed by a consonant, start the *v* early, on the pitch of the vowel before it, in this direction (◄—). In the phrase *love me*, sing the *v* on the pitch of the vowel *o*. Be careful not to add a vowel sound after the *v* (*lovah me*). Sing the m immediately after the *v* (*lovvme*).

---

*From *Collected Poems* by Elinor Wylie, published by Alfred A. Knopf, Inc.

Practice singing:

we strive to win	loves	our lives	(not *lies*)
save them	grieves	the leaves	(not *leas*)
it may grieve him	groves	he roves	(not *rows*)
believe me	believes	it moves	(not *moos*)

Oh, sleep, why dost thou leave me?
Again deceive me, oh sleep.

(Oh Sleep, Why Dost Thou Leave Me; Handel)

Or might I of Jove's nectar sup (not *Joe's*)

(Drink to Me Only with Thine Eyes; Ben Jonson)

Greensleeves was my heart of gold,
And who but my Lady Greensleeves?   (Eng. Folk Song)

v FOLLOWED BY *v* OR *f*

When a word ending in *v* is followed by a word beginning with *v* or *f*, connect the two words as if they were one longer word. In the first case, sing a long, continuous double *v*.
Practice:

to love virtue (*lovvirtue*)	they live forever (*livforever*)
we strive valiantly	love finds a way (*lovfinds*)
(*strivvaliantly*)	

v BEFORE A PAUSE

When *v* is followed by a pause, be careful not to add a vowel sound. Do not sing *while I livah*. Stop the voicing of the *v* before the lower lip leaves the upper teeth, not after, ending the word cleanly.
Practice singing:

. . . while I live —	. . . into the grave.
. . . how I grieve.	. . . we must leave;
What is love?	. . . the heavens above.

A SPECIAL NOTE ON *heav'n*

There are many songs in which the word *heaven* is written *heav'n*, and this contraction raises a special problem for the singer. The poet, needing a one-syllable word for his meter, has followed a convention by which the two-syllable *heaven* is made to look like a single syllable. The composer, in setting the poem, may have allotted only one note to *heav'n*, but the singer must avoid making it sound like a reference to poultry. (You have heard performances of *The Lost Chord* in which the singer informed you that "it may be that only in *Hen*, I shall hear that grand Amen.") The singer can maintain clarity in such instances by adding a tiny second syllable (*-ven*), provided that this syllable is added at the very end of the note. The vowel between *v* and *n* is a neutral vowel. (See Chapter 42.) For example:

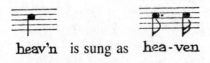

heav'n is sung as hea-ven

Sometimes, *heav'n* is written as a single syllable for more than one note. To maintain the composer's intention as well as the clarity of the word, add the tiny second syllable at the end of the last note. For example:

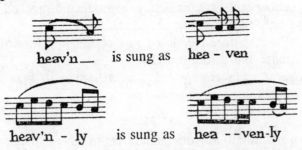

heav'n ‿   is sung as   hea - ven

heav'n - ly   is sung as   hea - -ven-ly

(*My Lovely Celia;* George Monro)

OF *of*

The preposition *of* is one of many incidental words — like *the, at, to, and,* etc. — that should not receive stress.

Emphasis on such words shifts attention from the meaning and poetry of a lyric. The effect is bound to be awkward and artificial.

The *v* sound in *of* must not be buzzed into prominence. It is to be treated casually. However, there is one isolated exception to this rule: When *of* is followed by *you,* the *v* should be sung with a vibrant, vocal sound. The reason for this is that "of you" almost invariably has some emotional connotation, and a well-buzzed *v* reinforces the expressive power.

Example:

I should forever dream of‿you. (*O, That It Were So;* Landor, Bridge)

13. *m* AND *n*

m is a voiced lip consonant with no voiceless partner. *n* is a voiced tongue-gum consonant with no voiceless partner. They are combined in one chapter because of many similarities in treatment.

ARTICULATION OF *m*

1. Hum *m* on a definite pitch with very relaxed lips.
   Do not tighten the lips.
2. The lips should be barely touching.
   Do not press the lips together tightly. Such pressure would either stifle *m* completely or produce a pinched tone.
3. Use only the inner surface of the lips.
   Do not turn the outer part of the lips inward, lest you tense the throat muscles.
4. In most instances, prolong *m* as though it were double *m*. (*My mother* is sung as *mmy mmother*.)

INITIAL *m*

The term "initial *m*" designates the *m* at the beginning of a word (*mine*) or syllable (*remain*). Naturally, initial *m* is always followed by a vowel.

After having hummed initial *m* as a double *m*, flip the lower lip away from the upper lip quickly and vigorously.

The humming and the flipping apart of the lips are equally essential. The first provides resonance; the second supplies projection and emphasis.

In the examples to be given, the sign < will represent the flipping apart of the lips.

There must be no separation between the *mm* and the vowel that follows it. They are closely connected.

Practice humming *mm* on various pitches. Then practice singing:

mm<ine	*mm<oan*
mm<eet	*mm<elt*
mm<ay	*mm<other*
mm<arch	*mm<oon*

56

ARTICULATION OF *n*

1. Intone *n* on a definite pitch while the tongue tip touches the upper gum.

2. Flatten the tip of the tongue against the gum.

> The tip of the tongue is flattened against the gum only for *n*. In sounding all other tongue-gum consonants, the tip of the tongue is <u>pointed</u> against the gum.

3. Keep the soft palate raised sufficiently to avoid excessive nasality. (The soft palate, which can be raised or lowered at will, is that part of the roof of the mouth back of the hard palate.)

> If the soft palate is lowered excessively, the tone will find its main channel through the nasal passage.

4. In most instances, prolong *n* as though it were double *n*. (*Night* is sung as *nnight*.)

INITIAL *n*

The term "initial *n*" designates the *n* at the beginning of a word (*name*) or syllable (*deny*). Naturally, initial *n* is always followed by a vowel.

After having intoned *n* as a double *n*, flip the tongue-tip downward from the gum quickly and vigorously. This action supplies projection and emphasis.

In the examples to be given, the sign ' will represent the flipping downward of the tongue.

There must be no separation between the *nn* and the vowel that follows it. They are closely connected.

Practice intoning *nn* on various pitches. Then practice singing:

nn'ame	*nn'ever*
nn'ight	*nn'ote*
nn'eed	*nn'one*
nn'ow	*nn'oon*

INITIAL *m* OR *n* BETWEEN VOWELS

The effective use of initial *m* or *n* between vowels is one of the most valuable devices for singing in English, and makes for:

1. Utmost clarity.
2. Smooth legato.
3. Vocal ease and resonance.
4. Expressiveness.

When an initial *m* or *n* occurs between two vowels (*be mine, thy name*), start the *mm* or *nn* in advance, in this direction (◄—).

The *mm* or *nn* is sung as the ending of the preceding word or syllable. "Steal time" from the preceding vowel (that is, shorten it), filling in the remainder of its note value with the hummed *mm* or intoned *nn*.

After having hummed *mm* thus, ahead of time, flip the lips apart directly to the following vowel. This second vowel is sung exactly in time, on the beat of the syllable in which it occurs. To effect this rhythmical accuracy, the lips flip apart exactly on the beat.

To illustrate, *be mine* is sung like this:

beemm—ine

The procedure with *nn* is the same, the tongue flipping exactly on the beat of the following vowel.

Thy name is sung like this:

thynn ame

TIME VALUES OF *mm* OR *nn*

How early should the *mm* or *nn* be sounded when it is sung ahead of time? For half the time value of the preceding vowel, as illustrated in the following tables:

Time Value of Preceding Vowel	When to Begin the *mm* or *nn*
Half note	On the second quarter
Quarter note	On the second eighth
Eighth note	On the second sixteenth
Sixteenth note	Practically immediately

There is an exception: When the preceding vowel has the value of a whole note, or of three quarter notes, begin the *mm* or *nn* on the last quarter. This will avoid exaggeration.

Remember that you will not be out of rhythm so long as you flip your lips or tongue to sing the vowel following *mm* or *nn* exactly on time.

Bear in mind that the *mm* or *nn* and the vowels that surround it are not separated, but, on the contrary, are closely connected. Practice singing:

be mine	(*beemm<ine*)	thy name	(*thynn'ame*)
to me	(*toomm<ee*)	by night	(*bynn'ight*)
no more	(*nomm<ore*)	my need	(*mynn'eed*)

A REMINDER ABOUT *r*

Because *r* is never sung before a consonant, it is, of course, omitted before *m* or *n*. Therefore, *m* or *n* between *r* and a vowel (*fo~~r~~ me, you~~r~~ name*) is actually *m* or *n* between vowels, and should be so sung.
Practice singing:

for me	(*fo~~r~~mm<ee*)	dear name	(*dea~~r~~nn'ame*)
her music	(*he~~r~~mm<usic*)	summer night	(*summe~~r~~nn'ight*)
you are mine	(*you ahmm<ine*)	you are near	(*you ahnn'ear*)
tormented	(*to~~r~~mm<ented*)	consternation	(*conste~~r~~nn'ation*)

INITIAL *m* OR *n* BETWEEN TWO VOWELS ON
TWO DIFFERENT PITCHES

The treatment of *m* or *n* in this situation is one of the important factors in expressive diction and must be a reliable part of the singer's equipment.

When either initial *m* or initial *n* occurs between two vowels that are not on the same pitch, sing the *m* or *n* on the pitch of the first vowel only, no matter which is higher or lower.
To illustrate:

NOTE: *m* and *n* differ in this respect from *v*.

    v between vowels is sung on whichever pitch is <u>lower</u> (←) or (→).

    m or *n* between vowels is sung on the pitch of the <u>first</u> vowel (←).

CAUTION

It is highly important that you take special care to sing the *m* or *n* on the pitch of the first vowel only. Singing it on the pitch of the second vowel would result in a distressing, gulping sound. Too often, singers do not listen to themselves sufficiently and make the mistake of singing *m* or *n* on the pitch of the wrong vowel.

Another even more serious error is to sing the *m* or *n* on the pitch of both vowels. This results in a scoop, probably the most unmusical and inartistic sound that can be emitted in singing.

But when *m* or *n* is sung correctly and accurately on the pitch of the first vowel only, it is extremely effective. As stated earlier in this chapter, it brings about perfect legato, clear enunciation, resonance of voice, and the effect of emotional warmth. For example, in *My Lovely Celia* by George Monro, when you sing "No more then torment me" with the *m* of *more* and of *torment* treated in the manner we have described, the emotional effect is greatly heightened. In the *Messiah,* when you sing "I know that my Redeemer liveth" with the *n* of *know* well anticipated, note how much this device contributes to the convincing fervor of the interpretation.

BRIEF SUMMARY OF DIRECTIONS FOR INITIAL *m* AND *n*

BETWEEN TWO VOWELS ON TWO DIFFERENT PITCHES

1. Hum *mm* with relaxed lips or *nn* with soft palate raised.
2. Start *mm* or *nn* ahead of the beat, stealing time from previous vowel. (**◄—**)
3. Sing *mm* or *nn* on preceding (first) pitch only.
4. Flip apart lips after *mm,* or flip tongue after *nn,* on the beat of the second vowel.
5. Connect *mm* or *nn* closely with vowels.

Practice singing the following phrases with the vowels before and after *m* or *n* on two different pitches. Sing each phrase twice, with first a rising then a falling interval:

be mine	(*beemm < ine*)	thy name	(*thynn'ame*)
to me	(*toomm < ee*)	by night	(*bynn'ight*)
no more	(*nomm < ore*)	they never	(*theynn'ever*)
blue moon	(*bluemm < oon*)	my need	(*mynn'eed*)
my mother	(*mmymm < other*)	you are near	(*you ahnn'ear*)
a memory	(*amm < emmory*)	you know	(*younn'ow*)
imagine	(*imm < agine*)	another	(*ann'other*)
tormented	(*to̶mm < ented*)	anointed	(*ann'ointed*)

Examples from vocal texts:

And suddenly, there was with the angel a *m*ultitude . . .
But there was no *m*an . . .
Why do the people i*m*agine a vain thing?
I k*n*ow that my Redee*m*er liveth.
Why do the *n*ations so furiously rage?   (*Messiah;* Handel)
Draw *n*ear, all ye people, come to *m*e. (*Elijah;* Mendelssohn)
Re*m*ember *m*e, but forget my fate. (*Dido and Aeneas;* Tate,
                                                        Purcell)
She *n*ever told her love (falling interval)
She *n*ever told her love (rising interval)
She sat, like patience on a *m*onu*m*ent.   (Shakespeare, Haydn)
No *m*ore then tor*m*ent me . . .
Where *m*elting beams so oft arise. (*My Lovely Celia;* Monro)
Songs my *m*other taught me . . .   (MacFarren, Dvořák)
*M*aybe he believes me, *m*aybe *n*ot. (*Maybe;* Sandburg, Kagen)
The winds of heaven mix forever
With a sweet e*m*otion.   (*Love's Philosophy;* Shelley, Quilter)
. . . and no soft throats
Yield their *m*usic to the *m*oon. (*The Green River;* Douglas,
                                                        Carpenter)

HIGH JUMPS MADE EASY

Sing an ascending interval of an octave, in the manner indicated,
selecting an octave that takes you to a high tone in your own range:

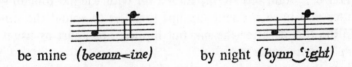

be mine *(beemm⸺ine)*   by night *(bynn ʿight)*

You will find that singing the *m* or *n* on the first note facilitates the
jump to the high note. The flipping of lips or tongue serves as an
easy springboard to the upper regions of the voice.

m OR *n* AFTER A CONSONANT

m or *n* after a consonant (*his mother, last night*) cannot be
sung ahead of time. There is no room for an anticipated *m* or *n*
when it is preceded by a consonant. Nor is there time for a double
m or double *n*. Merely sing a single *m* or *n* as the beginning of the
syllable in which it occurs and follow with a flip of lips or tongue
to the next vowel.

m OR *n* BEFORE A CONSONANT

An *m* or *n* before a consonant (as in *comfort* or *eventide*) is sung as *mm* or *nn* ahead of time. But there must be no vowel sound between the *mm* or *nn* and the consonant that follows it. (Do not sing *com-uh-fort* or *even-ah-tide*.)

To avoid an intervening vowel, observe the following precautions:

Do not flip the lips apart after *mm*, but keep them closed until you sound the next consonant.

Do not flip the tongue after *nn*, but hold it against the gum until you sound the next consonant.

Practice singing:

comfort	(*commfort*)	eventide	(*evenntide*)
implore	(*immplore*)	moonbeams	(*moonnbeams*)
some day	(*sommday*)	one day	(*wonnday*)
I am trembling	(*I ammtremmbling*)	green caves	(*greenncaves*)

m FOLLOWED BY *n*

n FOLLOWED BY *m*

When *m* and *n* follow each other in either order, there must be no intervening vowel sound. For example, do not sing *calm-ah-night* or *in-ah-mine*.

When *m* is followed by *n*, hum *mm* with lips closed until after you have placed the tongue against the gum in position to sound the *nn*. Do not flip the lips after the *mm*, but flip the tongue as usual after the *nn* (*calmmnn'ight*).

When *n* is followed by *m*, intone *nn* with tongue touching gum until after you have brought the lips together to sound the *mm*. Do not flip the tongue after the *nn*, but flip the lips apart as usual after the *mm* (*innmm<ine*).

When the two words occur on different pitches, sing both consonants on the pitch of the first.

calmmnn 'ight   *innmm—<ine*

Practice singing each phrase twice, with first a rising then a falling interval:

dream now	green meadow
come near	one man
Omnipotent	fine morning

m FOLLOWED BY *m*
n FOLLOWED BY *n*

When final *m* is followed by initial *m* (*from me*), or final *n* by initial *n* (*one night*), do not separate the words. Sing double *m* (*fromm<ee*) or double *n* (*wonn'ight*). When the two words occur on different pitches, sing the double consonant on the pitch of the first word.

Practice singing:

from me   one night
dream magic   a vision nears
Then shall the lame‿man leap as an hart.   (*Messiah*)
She will return‿no more. (*Lament of Ian the Proud;* MacLeod,
Griffes)

A SPECIAL NOTE ON THE PREFIX *un-*

In singing the prefix *un-*, much value must be given to the *n;* otherwise *unhappy, unfortunate* would sound like *a happy, a fortunate,* quite the opposite of their actual meaning. Sing the *n* as *nn,* well ahead of time. Take care, as usual, not to sound a vowel between the *nn* and the consonant that follows.

Practice singing:

unhappy   (*unnhappy*)   unknown   (*unnown*)
unfortunate   (*unnfortunate*)   unsung   (*unnsung*)

m OR *n* BEFORE A PAUSE

When either *m* or *n* occurs before a pause, there must be no additional vowel sound. Do not sing *going home-ah* or *she is mine-ah*.

Hum final *mm*, but stop the tone before the lips separate so that they may part silently.

Intone final *nn*, but stop the tone before the tongue leaves the gum so that the tongue may be released silently.

Practice singing:

We are going home.   She is mine.
I had a wondrous dream.   I am alone.

Call for the robin red breast and the wre*n* . . .
To rear him hillocks that shall keep him war*m*,
And (when gay tombs are robbed) sustain no har*m* . . .
But keep the wolf far thence, that's foe to me*n*,
For with his nails he'll dig them up agai*n*.

(*Dirge;* John Webster, Virgil Thomson)

14. WHEN TO SEPARATE WORDS

Up to this point, we have constantly stressed the importance of linking words together, and we shall continue to do so. However, we have learned from experience that this is the stage where singers ask questions about certain situations where words are <u>not</u> joined. We believe it useful, therefore, to defer momentarily the study of consonants and to name three specific situations in which words are separated. These are: (1) when a word ends in the same vowel sound that begins the next word; (2) when a word of importance might be mistaken for a different word; (3) when a word beginning with a vowel requires special emphasis for dramatic effect.

1. When a word ends in the same vowel sound that begins the next word, the words should be separated.
Examples:

Separate	Do Not Sing
three / eagles	*threeeagles*
*the / evil	*theevil*
*the / east	*theeast*
*the / evening	*theevening*
grow / open	*gropen*
so / old	"My mother is *sold*."

NOTE: It is only when the <u>sound</u> is identical, not the spelling, that the words are separated. When the sounds are unlike, there is no separation, even when the words are spelled with the same letter. Examples:

Do Not Separate
three elves
the end
the earth
no other
no one

---

*Remember that *the* before a vowel sound is pronounced as *thee*.

2. When a word of importance might be mistaken for a different word, the words should be separated.

Examples:

Separate	If Connected, the Second Word Would Seem to Be
bright / eyes	ties
big / eyes	guys
beautiful / eyes	lies
lasses' / eyes	size (or sighs)
deaf / ears	fears
watchful / ears	leers
my / ears	years
her / ear	rear
your / age	rage
good / aim	dame
some / others	mothers
quiet / isle	tile
white / orchard	tortured
name / any	many
are / aching	raking
cold / ashes	dashes
its / cares	scares

Further examples:

Let us / pray. (not *spray*)

Is it / I? (not *tie*)

You are / old. (not *rolled*)

If ice / melt . . . (not *I smelt*)

. . . or swan's down / ever. (not *never*)

(*Have You Seen But a White Lily Grow;* Ben Jonson)

The lass with the delicate / air. (not *tear*)

(Title of song by Arne)

. . . be light and / airy. (not *dairy*)

(*Shepherd! Thy Demeanour Vary;* Thomas Brown)

Sweet Little Buttercup / I! (not *pie*)

(*H.M.S. Pinafore;* Gilbert and Sullivan)

I who am / old . . . (not *mold*)

(*Lament of Ian the Proud;* MacLeod, Griffes)

In sweet music is such / art . . . (not *chart*)

(*Orpheus with His Lute;* Shakespeare, William Schuman)

So this winged / hour . . . (not *dower*)
. . . this inarticulate / hour. (not *tower*)
(Silent Noon; Rossetti, Vaughan Williams)
Sea nymphs / hourly ring his bell. (not *sourly*)
(Full Fathom Five Thy Father Lies; Shakespeare, Robert
Johnson)
NOTE: The singer must, of course, determine the importance or non-importance of words. By way of illustration, contrast the following phrases:

She walks in beauty (Byron). Here, the important words are *walks* and *beauty*. The word *in* is so unimportant that *walks in* can be connected without ambiguity or confusion of meaning.

Let us in. Here, the important word, the crux of the phrase, is *in*. If *us* is connected with *in*, the phrase will seem to be *Let us sin*. Therefore, in this phrase, *us* and *in* must be separated.

SPECIAL NOTE ON *eyes*

It is not usually necessary to separate *her eyes, your eyes,* or *their eyes*. The plural *eyes* and the singular *rise* will rarely be confused. In the following sentences, there is no suggestion of *rise:*

Her eyes are blue.
I gaze into your eyes.
Their eyes were full of tears.

REMINDER ABOUT *r* BEFORE A PAUSE

r is omitted before a pause. A separation between two words to avoid confusion of meaning is, in itself, a pause. Omit the *r* before the pause in phrases like the following:

you~~r~~ / age	you a~~r~~e / old
he~~r~~ / ear	their hearts a~~r~~e / aching

3. When a word beginning with a vowel requires special emphasis for dramatic effect, the words should be separated.
Examples:

my / endless misery
his / ill-fated journey
. . . if / aught but death

By this separation, the desired stress can be effected convincingly without recourse to the forcing that is sometimes substituted for genuine emotional power. Remember, however, that this device is only to be used for dramatic effect.

The following examples illustrate, first, a word occurring in a phrase where it should be connected, and then in a phrase where it should be separated for dramatic emphasis:

Connect	Separate for Dramatic Emphasis
I found her, just the other day.	Not this one, but the / *other* one.
My heart ever faithful . . . (Bach)	If / *ever* I find you, I shall have revenge.
They are all asleep.	Some are weak, but / *all* are guilty.
She has not gathered any flowers.	After such destruction, do / *any* remain?

15. *l*

The consonant *l* is voiced and has no voiceless partner.

In singing the consonant *l*, there are two techniques: one for initial *l* and one for final *l*. The terms "initial" and "final" are used in a special sense, and do not necessarily refer to *l* as the first or last letter of a word.

The term initial *l* designates the *l* before a vowel, as in *long* and *cloud*. Many words, such as *lovely*, have more than one initial *l*, one for each syllable.

The term final *l* designates the *l* after a vowel, as in *feel, all, smile, old, welcome*.

When *l* occurs between two vowels, it is sung as an initial *l*, on the pitch of the second vowel, starting the second syllable, in this direction (➤). For example: *feeling* is sung as *fee-ling, melody* as *me-lody*.

Double *l* is sung as a single *l*. For example, *billow* is sung as *bi-low*.

ARTICULATION OF INITIAL *l*

1. Flip the tongue tip down from the upper gum, quickly and vigorously, directly on the beat. Initial *l* moves in this direction (➤).

> The voicing of initial *l* should start at the instant when the tongue flips downward. Unlike *m* or *n*, initial *l* should not be prolonged or started ahead of the beat. A prolonged *l* before a vowel would mar the ensuing vowel and induce a throaty tone.
>
> Do not move the tongue slowly. It must be flipped rapidly. This does not imply that the vowel that follows is necessarily quick. The vowel may be of short or long duration, according to the music.

2. Point the tip of the tongue.

> Do not flatten the tongue tip as in pronouncing *n*.

3. Touch the gum well above the tooth line.

68

As a preliminary exercise, practice singing slowly:

la la   la la la la la la la la la la la

la   la la la la la   la   la

(This exercise is based on Carmen's scene with Zuniga in Act I, and will sound best if sung to Bizet's music. But for practice purposes, any sequence of notes can be used.)

Accent each underlined *la*. The accenting is accomplished by a more vigorous flip of the tongue; not by any sudden increase in volume, which might produce an inappropriate effect; and not by nodding the head, which would produce no effect at all! Now increase the speed of the exercise until it can be sung rapidly, always accenting the underlined *la*. The consonant in this underlined *la* is our initial *l*.

Practice singing, with a quick, vigorous *l*, followed by a long vowel sound:

love	Lord	lady	lone	lovely
light	lamb	long	linger	sadly
life	labor	lead	lose	brightly
laugh	lark	look	lost	sweetly

In practicing the following, flip the *l* between vowels as the beginning of the second syllable:

delightful	silent	calling	(*ca-ling*)
beloved	holy	willow	(*wi-low*)
believe	lily	yellow	(*ye-low*)
release	melody	smiling	(*smi-ling*)

Examples from vocal texts:

And He shall gather the *l*ambs with His arm . . . and gent*l*y *l*ead those that are with young . . . Come unto Him, all ye that *l*abour and are heavy *l*aden . . . and *l*earn of Him; for he is meek and *l*ow*l*y of heart.   (*Messiah;* Handel)

It is enough, O *L*ord, now take away my *l*ife . . . I desire to *l*ive no *l*onger; now *l*et me die.   (*Elijah;* Mendelssohn)

And *love* himself *lays* down his *lute* . . .
A *lovely lyric lady* . . .

> (*My Lady Walks in Loveliness;* Wood, Charles)

Do not go, my *love*, without asking my *leave* . . .
I fear *lest* I *lose* you, when I am *sleeping*.

> (*Do Not Go, My Love;* Tagore, Hageman)

My *love*, why have you *left* me a*lone?*

> (*I Hear An Army;* Joyce, Barber)

Lonely, ETC.

You have heard people sing, "None but the lone'y heart," or
"lowly heart" or "lone-ah-ly heart." To avoid the mistreatment of
lonely and similar words, sing *nn* ahead of the beat, with the tongue
tip slightly flattened against the gum; then, without removing the
tongue from the gum, bring it to a point and flip it quickly downward for the *l*.

Practice singing:

only	in love
lonely	on land
moonlight	green leaves
sunlight	one look

They on*ly live* who *life* enjoy. (*Preach Not Me;* Milton, Arne)

COMBINATION OF CONSONANT WITH *l*

A syllable beginning with a combination of two consonants, the
second of which is *l* (such as *please, blue, cloud*), is troublesome
for many singers. They sing *please* as *peas,* omitting the *l;* or as
leas, omitting the *p;* or as *puh-lease,* sounding a vowel between the
p and *l*.

Here is a valuable and easy device which will overcome the
difficulty:

Prepare the *l* by placing the tongue tip against the gum, first.
Then sound the two consonants simultaneously. The tongue flips
downward together with the sounding of the other consonant.

We can illustrate the procedure by printing the initial consonants

of the word *please* like this: $\left.{l\atop p}\right\}$ *ease.* We have written the *l* above

the *p* to indicate its geographical position in the mouth, and to
demonstrate that one consonant is not sounded before the other.
Sung in this manner, both consonants are equally clear, and there
is no intervening vowel.

Practice singing:

blue	cloud	flame	glow	please
blame	clasp	flower	gleam	play
blind	clear	fly	glory	plead
blush	close	flight	gloom	plight
bleak	cling	flew	glisten	plume
black	proclaim	flee	glance	plan
oblivion	recline	reflect	glass	reply
nobly	darkly	gruffly	ugly	hopeless

NOTE: Syllables beginning with *sl* cannot be pronounced in this manner. The tongue cannot be in two places at once! In words like *slow, sleep,* etc., pronounce first *s,* then *l.*

Examples from vocal texts:

. . . and the rough *pl*aces *pl*ain . . . Then shall the eyes of the b*l*ind be opened . . .   (*Messiah;* Handel)

And the thunder of horses *pl*unging . . .

They *cl*eave the *gl*oom of dreams, a b*l*inding *fl*ame,

*Cl*anging upon the heart as upon an anvil.

(*I Hear an Army;* Joyce, Barber)

FINAL *l*

To re-state our definition, the term final *l* designates the *l* after a vowel, as in *feel, all, smile, old, welcome.*

ARTICULATION OF FINAL *l*

1. Sing final *l* (unlike initial *l*) ahead of time, in this direction (◄—). While singing the preceding vowel, touch the tip of the tongue to the upper gum, continuing the vocal sound.

2. The tongue must not touch the gum too early, but only toward the end of the preceding vowel. The observance of this principle is essential to good tone quality.

3. Keep the soft palate high.

4. There is no flip of the tongue after final *l.* This is highly important, because there must be no accidental vowel sound after final *l.*

Do not sing *all-uh* for *all,* or *wel-uh-come* for *welcome,* or *will-uh come* for *will come.*

Practice singing:

all	smile	help	hills	welcome	all night
small	isle	melt	bells	altar	will cry
tell	soul	guilt	halls	elder	dull days
fill	whole	wild	miles	hilltop	full measure
kill	goal	mild	skulls	children	tall trees

Examples from vocal texts:

Preach not me your musty ru*l*es,
Ye drones that mou*l*d in id*l*e ce*ll*,
The heart is wiser than the schoo*l*s,
The senses a*l*ways reason we*ll*.

(*Air* from *Comus;* Milton, Arne)

Pi*l*e the bodies high at Austerlitz and Waterloo,
Shove*l* them under and let me work —
I am the grass; I cover a*ll*.

(*Grass;* Carl Sandburg,* Frederic Hart)

SPECIAL CAUTION: *ool, eel, ale*

Take care not to distort the vowel sounds *oo*, *ee*, and *ay*, when they precede *l*. Do not, for example, sing *coo-el* for *cool, fee-ul* for *feel,* or *day-ul* for *dale.* To avoid this undesirable effect, move the tongue tip up to the gum quickly at the instant when the *l* should be sounded. Do not cause the tongue to arrive there gradually.

Practice singing:

cool	feel	dale
pool	heal	pale
fool	steal	vale
school	seal	fail
rule	kneel	hail

SPECIAL CAUTION: *ode* AND *old*

Sound the *l* sufficiently to distinguish between the words given below. (Do not sing "He towed me" for *He told me.*)

ode - old	towed - told	feed - field
goad - gold	word - world	weed - wield

But I'm for right Jamaica
Till I roll beneath the bench
Says the *old bold* mate of Henry Morgan.

(*Captain Stratton's Fancy;* Masefield,** Deems Taylor)

---

*From *Cornhuskers* by Carl Sandburg. Copyright, 1918, by Henry Holt & Co., Inc.
**John Masefield's *Captain Stratton's Fancy,* copyright, 1912, by The Macmillan Company; copyright renewed, 1940. Used by permission.

SILENT *l*

Many singers often forget that *l* is a silent letter, spelled but not
sounded, in such words as the following:

walk	alms	psalm	calf
talk	balm	qualms	half
stalk	calm	folk	calves
chalk	palm	yolk	halves

FINAL *l* FOLLOWED BY A WORD BEGINNING WITH A VOWEL

When final *l* is followed by a word beginning with a vowel, treat
it as an initial *l*. It is flipped as the beginning of the second word,
moving in this direction (→).

Practice singing:

steal away	(*stea-laway*)	full of	(*fu-lof*)
tell us	(*te-lus*)	all our	(*a-lour*)

Yet *will ͜ I* love her *till ͜ I* die.

(*I Know a Lady;* Thomas Ford, many settings)

Have you seen but the *fall ͜ of* the snow . . .

Have you felt the *wool ͜ of* beaver . . .

(*Have You Seen But a White Lily Grow;* Ben Jonson)

FINAL *l* FOLLOWED BY INITIAL *l*

When final *l* is followed by initial *l*, as in the phrase *all lovers,*
pronounce both, without separating them. The final *l* of *all* is sung
as part of the preceding vowel, in this direction (←); the tongue
tip remains against the gum momentarily, then is flipped to pronounce the initial *l* of *lovers,* in this direction (→). The tongue
does not leave the gum between the words, and no actual separation
occurs.

Practice singing:

all lovers	dull light	her smile lingers
cool lake	well loved	evil look

My *whole ͜ life* long . . .

(*Night Song at Amalfi;* Teasdale, Naginski)

Silence will *fall ͜ like* dews . . .

(*Velvet Shoes;* Wylie, Thompson)

16. *k* AND "HARD" *g*

k (voiceless) and *g*, as in *go* (voiced), constitute a pair of consonants articulated through contact between the back of the tongue and the soft palate. This *g* is sometimes called "hard" *g* in contrast to "soft" *g* as in *George*.

k

For convenience, the phonetic symbol [k] will be used to represent all spellings of this sound. The spellings are:

> *k* as in *king*
>
> *c* as in *cool*
>
> *ck* as in *back*
>
> *q* as in *quiet*
>
> *ch* as in *choir*

ARTICULATION OF [k]

1. Raise the back of the tongue to meet the soft palate at the highest point possible.

> Do not substitute *h* for [k]. Failure to make contact between the back of the tongue and the soft palate eliminates the *k* sound and substitutes *h*.
>
> The effect would be:
>
> > "Hum unto me" for *Come unto me*.
> >
> > > (*Messiah;* Handel)
> >
> > "Nymphs and shepherds, hum away" for *come away*.
> >
> > > (*Nymphs and Shepherds;* Shadwell, Purcell)
> >
> > "I hear you hauling me" for *calling me*.
> >
> > > (*I Hear You Calling Me;* Harford, Marshall)
> >
> > If the back of the tongue and the soft palate meet at too low a point, the effect would be a gargling sound resembling the clearing of the throat.

2. From the point of contact between the back of the tongue and the soft palate, blow a stream of air sufficient to be audible.

> Do not substitute *g* for [k] by voicing the consonant instead of blowing a stream of air. The effect would be:

74

"Gum unto me" for *Come unto me.*
"Nymphs and shepherds, gum away."
"I hear you galling me."

See what can happen when *g* is substituted for final *k!*

"Carry me bag to old Virginny" for *Carry me back.*

(James Bland)

Do not substitute an imploded [k] for an exploded [k]. A [k] is imploded when the contact between tongue and soft palate causes a stop without an explosion of air. The result is an inaudible [k] and a stop that breaks the musical line with no apparent justification. The effect would be:

"Tay' / His yo' / upon thee" for *Take His yoke upon thee.* (*Messiah*)

3. Blow the stream of air forward; expel it well out of the mouth.

Do not hold back the aspiration within the mouth. The result would be a blocked-up [k] which, when followed by a vowel, would constrict the tone. When the air is blown outward, the [k] is clear and the following vowel can be projected freely.

DO NOT OMIT [k]

Singers sometimes ignore [k], not because of faulty technique, but through simple negligence. Do not omit [k]. The effect would be:

"ween" for *queen*   "loud" for *cloud*
"wyet" for *quiet*   "ool" for *cool*
"leer" for *clear*   "dring" for *drink*
"Um unto me" for *Come unto me.*

*   *

*

Before practicing the words given below, it should be pointed out that a well aspirated [k] enhances not only clarity, but also descriptive and expressive potentialities. The explosion of air gives to *cool* and *cold* a chilly sound; it gives to *quiet* a hushing effect; it gives to *quick, clear, click* a characteristic crispness.

Practice singing:

cool	*clear	walk	drink
cold	clean	talk	think
quiet	close	like	wink
queen	cloud	back	brink
care	click	seek	ask
courage	cloak	spoke	task
choir	clock	awake	flask
kind	quick	invoke	work
king	crack	music	silk

Comfort ye, my people . . . Spea*k* ye *c*omfortably to Jerusalem and *c*ry unto her that her warfare is a*cc*omplished, that her ini*q*uity is pardoned . . . Behold, thy *k*ing *c*ometh unto thee.   (*Messiah*)

For the *c*all of the running tide
Is a wild *c*all and a *c*lear *c*all . . .
And all I as*k* is a windy day with the white *c*louds flying . . .
(*Sea Fever;* Masefield, Ireland)

The winter is *c*rying "Sleep no more."
My *k*iss will give peace now
And *q*uiet to your heart.   (*Sleep Now;* Joyce, Barber)

How to Connect [k]

[k] before a vowel

When [k] is followed by a word or syllable beginning with a vowel, use the [k] as a connecting link, sounding it as the beginning of the next syllable or word. The [k] moves in this direction (➤). Practice singing:

waken	(*wa-ken*)	wake us	(*wa-kus*)
speaketh	(*spea-keth*)	speak of	(*spea-kof*)
taking	(*ta-king*)	take it	(*ta-kit*)

And he shall feed his flo*ck* like‿a shepherd . . . Ta*k*e his yo*k*e‿upon you . . . For he is mee*k*‿and lowly of heart. Thy rebu*k*e hath bro*k*en his heart.   (*Messiah;* Handel)

Is not his word . . . li*k*e‿a hammer that brea*k*eth a ro*ck*‿into pieces?   (*Elijah;* Mendelssohn)

Let us wal*k*‿in the white snow . . .
With footsteps *q*uiet and slow,
At a tran*q*uil pace . . .   (*Velvet Shoes;* Wylie, Thompson)

---

*Remember to prepare the tongue first for the *l*, and to sound the *c* and *l* simultaneously, as described on page 70.

[k] BEFORE A CONSONANT

Special Directions for [kt]

For convenience, we shall use the phonetic symbols [kt] to represent the various spellings of this sound. The spellings are:

-*ct* as in *act*
-*ked* as in *evoked*
-*cked* as in *bedecked*

Many singers are conspicuously careless in pronouncing [kt]. They sing, "you a't" (*you act*) and "he axe" (*he acts*); "Why dost thou affli't us?" (*afflict us*) and "he afflix us" (*afflicts us*), etc.

To sing [kt] correctly, first practice whispering *k* - - - - *t, k* - - - - *t,* slowly, and with an explosion of air after each consonant. Then, still whispering, and still aspirating each consonant, gradually increase the speed until the *k* and *t* are close together:

k - - - *t, k* - - - *t, k* - - *t, k* - - *t, k-t, k-t, kt, kt, kt.*

Now, sing *act,* using voice for the vowel, but whispering the [kt]. This is the correct way to sing this word. Note that there should be no vowel sound after either the [k] or the *t.*

Practice singing:

act	evoked	bedecked	victory
afflict	liked	wrecked	nectar
reject	worked	wracked	picture (not *pitcher*)
conflict	walked	winked	asked (not *ast*)
distract	talked	blinked	basked

He was despised and reje*ct*ed.   (*Messiah*)
And turn from their sin when Thou dost affli*ct* them . . . Go up again and still loo*k t*oward the sea . . . Have respe*ct* to the prayer of Thy servant . . .   (*Elijah*)
Drin*k t*o me only with thine eyes . . .
But might I of Jove's nec*t*ar sup . . .
(*Drink to Me Only with Thine Eyes;* Ben Jonson)

Special Directions for [kts]

The combination [kts], as in *acts,* should be practiced by pronouncing first *k,* then *ts.* This is the *ts* sound described on page 37 in discussing *rests.* Whisper slowly: *k* - - - - *ts, k* - - - - - *ts;* then with gradually increasing speed until the two sounds are close together: *k - - - ts, k - - ts, k-ts, kts.*

Practice, singing the vowels, but whispering the [kts]:

acts	rejects
facts	directs
afflicts	collects
conflicts	distracts

[k] BEFORE OTHER CONSONANTS AND BEFORE A PAUSE

[k] before other consonants is pronounced with the technique described above: a whispered, aspirated sound, close to the follow-ing consonant, and with no intervening vowel sound. Before a pause, also, take care not to add a vowel sound.

Practice singing:

darkness	forsake him
wakeful	like those
asks	ask for
tasks	seek me (not *see me*)

He shall spea*k* peace . . . For behold, dar*k*ness shall *c*over the earth.
(Messiah; Handel)

If with all your hearts ye truly see*k* me . . .
(Elijah; Mendelssohn)

But let *c*oncealment li*k*e a worm in the bud
Feed on her damas*k* chee*k*.
(She Never Told Her Love; Shakespeare, Haydn)

I shall go shod in sil*k* . . .
White as a white *c*ow's mil*k* . . .
(Velvet Shoes; Wylie, Thompson)

FINAL [k] BEFORE ANOTHER [k]

When final [k] is followed by a word beginning with [k], the repetition of the consonant would make an unpleasant effect. This is one of the rare instances in which implosion is used. Implode the first [k] (that is, stop the consonant without exploding it) and ex-plode the second [k].

Practice singing:

speak quietly	take courage
invoke compassion	walk quickly

"HARD" *g*

The consonant *g* (as in *go*) is commonly known as "hard" *g*. It is the voiced consonant corresponding to voiceless [k].

For "soft" *g* (as in *George*), see Chapter 26. For the combined letters *ng* (as in *sing*), see Chapter 20.

ARTICULATION OF HARD *g*

Raise the back of the tongue to meet the soft palate at the highest point possible, and as tongue and palate separate, add voice.

Do not substitute an explosion of air for the voicing of *g*. The result would be [k].

Practice singing:

go	guide	green
gain	guilt	gray
glow	grow	groan

HOW TO CONNECT HARD *g*

HARD *g* BEFORE A VOWEL

When a syllable or word ending in *g* is followed by a syllable or word beginning with a vowel, use the *g* as a connecting link, sounding it as the beginning of the next syllable or word. The *g* moves in this direction (➤).

Practice singing (note that double *g* is sung as one *g*):

tiger	(*ti-ger*)	beg us	(*be-gus*)
bigger	(*bi-ger*)	the bag of the bee	(*ba-gof*)
beggar	(be-*gar*)	the plague of love	(*pla-gof*)

HARD *g* BEFORE A CONSONANT AND BEFORE A PAUSE

The treatment of final *g* before a consonant or before a pause is covered in the following chapter.

17. FINAL *b,* *d,* AND "HARD" *g*

In the preceding chapters we have cautioned the singer against allowing any extraneous vowel sound to be heard after a final consonant when it is followed by a word beginning with a consonant, and when it occurs before a pause.

Now, however, we shall discuss three consonants which, when final, are exceptions to the general rule against inserting vowel sounds where none exist in the text. These three final consonants — and only these three — require special treatment by the addition of a vowel sound.

These three consonants are *b, d,* and what is sometimes known as "hard" *g.* This is the *g* in the word *beg* and is represented in the phonetic alphabet by the symbol [g]. (It is not to be confused with "soft" *g,* as in *George,* which is represented in the phonetic alphabet by the symbol [dʒ].)

> Final *b,* final *d,* and final hard *g* must be followed by a light vowel sound approximating -*uh* when they occur before a consonant or before a pause.

These three consonants — only these three — are completely inaudible unless they are followed by a vowel sound. If there is no vowel sound following these consonants in the text, the singer must supply the necessary sound. Try to sing *b, d,* or hard *g* without an additional vowel sound. The result will be silence. If you explode these consonants, you will be substituting their voiceless partners: *p, t,* and *k.*

To illustrate for yourself the effects outlined in the preceding paragraph, sing the words *sob, maid,* and *beg* without an additional vowel sound. You will be singing "sah," "may," and "beh." Then, if you attempt to remedy this loss of final consonant by aspirating it, you will bring about some strange corruptions of text. *Sob* will become *sop, maid* will be changed into *mate,* and *beg* will become *beck.*

DIRECTIONS FOR SINGING VOWEL SOUND AFTER
FINAL *b*, *d*, AND HARD *g*

1. Sing a light vowel sound approximating -*uh* after final *b*, *d*, and hard *g*.

2. Sing this light vowel sound as a short additional syllable approximating an additional 32nd note.

3. Sing this additional vowel sound on the identical pitch of the word ending in *b*, *d*, or hard *g*.

> Do not sing the additional vowel on a lower pitch. This would result in something like a resonant symptom of dyspepsia.

To illustrate the effective manner of singing these final consonants:

Here is a simple if unesthetic device for remembering *b*, *d*, and hard *g*: they are the consonants in the word *bedbug*.

FINAL *b* AND FINAL HARD *g*

Only a few words ending in *b* or hard *g* are found in vocal literature. Those most frequently sung are given below.

Practice singing the following words ending in *b* and *g* with a light additional -*uh* sound on the identical pitch of each one:

sob	We hear them sob.
rob	Do not rob them.
robe	He wore a golden robe.
web	The web caught him.
beg	I beg forgiveness.

bag   He found a bag laden with silver.
dig   We dig below.
dog   The dog bays at the moon.

plague   The pleasing plague stole on me!

(The Plague of Love; Arne)

FINAL *d*

Words ending in *d* are frequently found in vocal literature. It is in these words especially that the omission of final *d* or the substitution of *t* for *d* alters the sense ("mine" for *mind*, "he will fine me" for *he will find me*, "write" for *ride*, etc.). Words ending in *d* also include the past tense of hundreds of verbs ending in voiced consonants (*dreamed, loved, found,* etc.). The omission of final *d* in these words disturbs the listener by confusing the present tense with the past.

Practice singing, with a light *-uh* sound on the identical pitch of the word or syllable ending in *d:*

find	(not *fine*)	fade	(not *fate*)
mind	(not *mine*)	feed	(not *feet*)
lord	(not *law*)	dead	(not *debt*)
hold	(not *whole*)	pined	(not *pint*)
bold	(not *bowl*)	grand	(not *grant*)
maid	(not *may*)	maid	(not *mate*)
ride	(not *rye*)	ride	(not *write*)
rode	(not *row*)	rode	(not *wrote*)
side	(not *sigh*)	side	(not *sight*)
field	(not *feel*)	stayed	(not *state*)
kind	(not *kine*)	abide	(not *a bite*)
tide	(not *tie*)	tide	(not *tight*)

sound	sword	old	dreamed	kindness
ground	wide	told	died	find them
hand	confide	gold	dared	beside me
land	greed	word	loved	told him
husband	behold	world	found	rode forth

He shall fee*d* his flock, like a shepher*d* . . . They were sore afrai*d* . . . But who may abi*d*e the day of his coming? And who shall stan*d* when he appeareth?   (*Messiah;* Handel)

Where e'er you walk, cool gales shall fan the gla*d*e . . .
Where e'er you trea*d* . . .

(Where E'er You Walk, from Semele; Handel)

Ye shall ever surely fin*d* me . . . Thou art Lor*d* Go*d* . . . Let
their hearts again be turne*d* . . . Now behol*d*, thy son liveth.

(*Elijah*, Mendelssohn)

There is a lady sweet and kin*d*,
Was never face so please*d* my min*d*.

(*There Is a Lady;* Thomas Ford, many settings)

FOUR EXCEPTIONS IN WHICH FINAL *d*
IS NOT EMPHASIZED

There are four exceptions in which final *d* should not be followed by an additional vowel sound:

1. After the word *and*.
> The word *and* is merely a conjunction, a connective that
> should not be made prominent.

Examples:

day and‿night	joy and‿happiness
father and‿mother	the moon and‿the sea

. . . and‿merciful and‿kind and‿gracious.   (*Elijah*)
It was a lover and‿his lass . . .   (Shakespeare, Morley)

In phrases like *you and I,* the *d* must be extremely light to avoid
confusion with *die*.

2. When the next word begins with *r* or *s*.
Examples:

To whom is the arm of the Lord‿revealed?   (*Elijah*)
Thy sting is not so sharp
As friend‿remembered not.

    (*Blow, Blow, Thou Winter Wind;* Shakespeare, Quilter)
And‿God‿said . . .   (*The Creation;* Haydn)
Cease, O my sad‿soul.   (Purcell)

**3. After auxiliary verbs when they are followed by another
word.**
In the examples below, the auxiliary verbs are in italics:

could‿try
would‿go
should‿bring
had‿found
did‿bless
My love and I *did*‿meet. (*Down by the Sally Gardens;* Yeats,
trad.)

When auxiliary verbs occur before a pause, they are more emphatic in meaning, and, in that case, are followed by the additional light vowel sound.

Examples:

If only I could!

I know that I would! etc.

4. After the words _good, bad,_ and _glad_ when they are followed by another word.

Examples:

good‿bye	bad‿times	glad‿times
good‿night	bad‿tidings	glad‿tidings
good‿morrow	bad‿luck	glad‿moments
good‿luck	bad‿thoughts	gladness

. . . and bring glad‿tidings of good‿things.   (_Messiah_)

When the words _good, bad,_ and _glad_ occur before a pause, follow them with the additional light vowel sound.

Examples:

It is good.

They were bad.

We are glad.

*   *

*

FINAL _b_ FOLLOWED BY INITIAL _b_

When final _b_ is followed by a word beginning with _b,_ both consonants should be sounded only when the music is very slow.

Practice singing, first slowly, then quickly:

They sob bitterly.

We rob boldly.

The web broke.

FINAL _d_ FOLLOWED BY INITIAL _d_
FINAL HARD _g_ FOLLOWED BY INITIAL HARD _g_

When final _d_ is followed by a word beginning with _d,_ or when final _g_ is followed by a word beginning with _g,_ one _d_ or one _g_ is generally sufficient for both words.

Examples:

send down	(_sen-down_)	they beg greedily	(_be-greedily_)
loud drum	(_lou-drum_)	a big girl	(_bi-girl_)
fond dreams	(_fon-dreams_)	the dog growls	(_do-growls_)

Only when the first word might be misunderstood, is there any

necessity for an additional vowel sound after its final consonant.
Examples:

The maid deserts him might sound like *The May deserts him.*
The shade draws near might sound like *The shay draws near.*
The plague grows might sound like *The play grows.*

FINAL *b, d,* OR HARD *g* BEFORE A WORD
BEGINNING WITH A VOWEL

This chapter has dealt with final *b, d,* and *g* before a word beginning with a consonant and before a pause, and the need for an added vowel sound, in these circumstances, has been explained. However do not insert an additional vowel when final *b, d,* or *g* is followed by a word beginning with a vowel. Connect the two words by singing the *b, d,* or *g* as the beginning of the second word. The consonant moves in this direction (➤).

Practice singing:

Do not rob us.   (*ro-bus*)
The web is broken.   (*we-bis*)

He may find it.   (*fin-dit*)
They sat beside us.   (*besi-dus*)
Sound an alarm.   (*soun-dan*)

We beg of you.   (*be-gof*)
He dug underneath.   (*du-gunderneath*)
Out of the land of the living. (*lan-dof*)   (*Messiah*)
Shall the dead arise? (*dea-darise*)   (*Elijah*)
Trees where you sit shall crowd into a shade. (*crow-dinto*)
                        (*Where E'er You Walk;* Handel)
Journeys end in lovers meeting . . . (*en-din*)
                        (*O Mistress Mine;* Shakespeare, Quilter)
The tide is full . . . (*ti-dis*)
We find also in the sound a thought . . . (*fin-dalso*) (*soun-da*)
                        (*Dover Beach;* Matthew Arnold, Barber)

FINAL *b, d,* OR HARD *g* BEFORE INITIAL *w* OR *y*

Do not insert an additional vowel when final *b, d,* or *g* is followed by a word beginning with *w* or *y.* Connect the two words by singing the *b, d,* or *g* as the beginning of the second word, moving in this direction (➤).

Practice singing:

they sob wildly	(*so-bwildly*)	to rob your nest	(*ro-byour*)
red wine	(*re-dwine*)	beside you	(*besi-dyou*)
big waves	(*bi-gwaves*)	we beg you	(*be-gyou*)
Abide with me . . .	(*abi-dwith*)		(Lyte, Monk)
Ye people, rend your hearts . . .	(*ren-dyour*)	(*Elijah;* Mendels-	
			sohn)

18. *th*

In singing, *th* must be articulated more carefully than in our daily speech. In ordinary conversation, *th* is usually pronounced with the tip of the tongue inside the teeth. But when speaking or singing from a platform or even through a microphone, this kind of *th* does not project sufficiently; nor is it expressive.

ARTICULATION OF *th*

1. Before sounding *th*, place the tongue tip just outside of and lightly touching the edges of the upper front teeth.

> Extend only the very tip of the tongue. Anything more would be awkward for singing and might be regarded as a disrespectful gesture to your audience.

2. Form the tongue tip into its thinnest possible shape. A thick tongue is unmanageable and muffles the consonantal sound.

3. Draw the tongue tip quickly inward, rubbing it against the edges of the upper front teeth.

> The word "quickly" is important, because a slow tongue action impairs clarity. But this quick tongue action does not affect the duration of any vowel that may precede or follow.

4. Keep the lower teeth out of the way, or there may be an accident!

> A lacerated tongue is defective singing equipment; and even where there is no physical damage, no agreeable sound can come through clenched teeth.

TWO KINDS OF *th*

There are two kinds of *th*: voiceless (as in *thin*) and voiced (as in *thine*). The tongue action is identical for both. The only difference between them is implied in their designations: voiceless *th* and voiced *th*.

VOICELESS *th* (AS IN *thin*)

To articulate voiceless *th* (as in *thin*), blow out a stream of air while the tongue is being drawn inward. Since there is no voice in this consonant, the stream of air must be strong enough to be audi-

87

ble. This is of especial importance when voiceless *th* occurs at the end of a word, because these words may have dramatic importance, and they are completely incomprehensible without the *th*.
Practice, first whispering, then singing each word:

thin	thank	death	worth
through	think	earth	dearth
throng	thought	birth	wreath
thirty	thistle	wrath	both
thirsty	thousand	wroth	bath
three	thief	breath	path

Examples from vocal texts:

The *th*irst that from the soul doth rise . . .

(*Drink to Me Only with Thine Eyes;* Ben Jonson)

I kneel and *th*ank the gods for their assistance.

But what avails this *th*read of mere existence?

(Recit. *Hear Me Ye Winds and Waves,* from *Julius Caesar;* Handel)

A *th*ousand, *th*ousand sighs to save . . .

(*Come Away, Death;* Shakespeare, Quilter)

I never *th*ought of *th*inking for myself at all.

(*When I Was a Lad,* from *H.M.S. Pinafore;* Gilbert and Sullivan)

VOICED *th* (AS IN *thine*)

To articulate voiced *th* (as in *thine*), add voice, instead of blowing out a stream of air, while the tongue is being drawn inward.

Sing the phrases *to thee* and *I am thine* with this method of articulation and hear the added resonance and emotional color.
Practice singing:

thine	thy	these
thee	thus	though
thou	those	thence

Examples from vocal texts:

I would not change for *th*ine.   (*Drink to Me Only*)

Oh, *th*ou that tellest good tidings to Zion . . .

Behold, *th*y king cometh unto *th*ee . . .   (*Messiah*)

*Th*ough *th*ey are by Him redeemed . . . . (*Elijah*)

Dearest, *th*ere to dream of *th*ee . . .

(*By a Lonely Forest Pathway;* transl. Chapman, Griffes)

EXCEPTION: THE ARTICLE *the*

Do not emphasize the article *the*. Here is one *th* that should not be projected, *the* being a word of no importance. The stress belongs on the word that follows it; otherwise the phrase becomes stilted and artificial.

PRONUNCIATION OF THE PREPOSITION *with*

In singing the preposition *with,* we prefer the voiced *th,* although in speech, the word may properly be pronounced with either a voiced or voiceless ending. We prefer the voiced *th* because: (1) a preposition should be unstressed; and (2) the voiced *th* produces a smoother legato. The explosiveness of voiceless *th* would give this word more prominence than a preposition should have. The word following *with* is always the more important of the two. When voicing *th* in *with,* do not emphasize it.

The same principle applies when *with* is part of a compound word (*without, within, withal*). Use the voiced *th.*

Practice singing:

with me	with us	without
with gladness	with honor	within
with beauty	with anger	withal

A man of sorrow and acquainted with grief . . .   (*Messiah*)
If with all your hearts . . .   (*Elijah*)

with BEFORE ANOTHER *th*

When *with* is followed by a word beginning with *th,* omit the *th* of *with* entirely. Sing only the *th* that begins the second word. The kind of *th* to be sung is determined by the kind of *th* that starts the second word.

Practice singing:

Voiceless *th*		Voiced *th*	
with thanks	(*wi-thanks*)	with thee	(*wi-thee*)
with thorns	(*wi-thorns*)	with thine	(*wi-thine*)
with thirst	(*wi-thirst*)	with these	(*wi-these*)
with thunder	(*wi-thunder*)	with those	(*wi-those*)
with threats	(*wi-threats*)	with thy	(*wi-thy*)

Drink to me only with thine eyes . . . (*wi-thine*)

(Ben Jonson)

And with thy love, ease my troubled mind. (*wi-thy*)

(*My Lovely Celia;* George Monro)

n OR *l* BEFORE *th*

Singers sometimes find it difficult to avoid inserting a vowel sound between words in such phrases as *in thee* and *all thoughts.*

They sing *in-a-thee* and *all-a-thoughts*. Here is an easy device for overcoming each of these difficulties.

n BEFORE *th*

Speak the word *month*, with the tongue tip placed outside of and touching the edges of the upper front teeth to form the *th*. Observe that while the tongue tip is extended outside in preparation for the *th*, you can sound the *n* by resting the blade of the tongue (that section just behind the tip) against the gum. It is not necessary to move the tongue tip twice: first against the gum for *n*, and then outside of the upper teeth for *th*. One tongue motion is sufficient for both *n* and *th*, and the consonants are closely joined without an intervening vowel sound.

Apply this same technique when one word ends in *n* and the next begins with *th*, whether voiceless (*one thought*) or voiced (*in thee*). Place the tip of the tongue outside of and touching the edges of the upper front teeth; sound the *n* with the blade of the tongue; then sound the *th* while drawing the tongue tip inward.

Practice singing:

	Voiceless *th*	Voiced *th*
month	ten thousand	in thee
seventh	vain things	when thou
ninth	serene thoughts	upon these
tenth	one thief	even thus

Examples from vocal texts:

One‿thought of thee all other thought drives from me.

                 (*I Love Thee, Dear;* transl. H. G. Chapman, Grieg)

The glory of the Lord is risen upo*n*‿*th*ee.   (*Messiah*)

O show to all these people that I have do*ne*‿*the*se things . . .

I will strengthe*n*‿*th*ee . . .   (*Elijah*)

l BEFORE *th*

There is a counterfeit *l* which should be used only before *th*. Here it will sound normal, but its unorthodox pronunciation would be noticeable in any other situation. This special *l* is used when one word ends in *l* and the next begins with *th*, whether voiceless (*all thoughts*) or voiced (*all thine*), and, of course, in words ending in *-lth*, such as *health*. We shall illustrate the articulation of this counterfeit *l* in the word *health*. Speak this word in the following manner:

First, place your tongue tip outside of and touching the edges of your upper front teeth; sound the *l* in this position; then draw

the tongue tip inward for the *th*. One motion of the tongue is sufficient. There is no intervening vowel sound.
Practice singing:

Voiceless *th*		Voiced *th*
health	all thoughts	I am all thine
wealth	evil things	we call thee
stealth	steal through	tell them
	feel thirst	although

Examples from vocal texts:
Sleep, my love, and peace attend thee
All‿*th*rough the night.
>   (*All Through the Night;* Boulton, Old Welsh Air)
Thou shalt love Him with all‿*th*ine heart . . .   (*Messiah*)
The common fate of all‿*th*ings rare
May read in thee . . .   (*Go, Lovely Rose;* Waller, Quilter)

ARTICULATION OF THE VOICELESS ENDING: -*ths*

In pronouncing the plural or possessive voiceless ending: -*ths*
(as in *faiths* or *faith's*), do not omit the *th*. Many singers carelessly
pronounce this as *face, deaths* as *dess*, etc.
    As a preliminary exercise, whisper the word *thistle,* several times.
Now sing *fai-* and whisper *thistle,* several times.
    Then sing *fai-* and whisper only the first syllable of *thistle*. This
is how the word *faiths* should be sung.
Practice singing, in the same manner:

faiths	heaths
death's	wraith's
myths	births
hearth's	earth's

Deep in the sun-searched *growths* . . .
>   (*Silent Noon;* D. G. Rossetti, Vaughan Williams)

SPECIAL NOTE ON *months* AND *depths*

The words *months* and *depths* are frequently mispronounced,
becoming *monss* and *depss* (and even *depsth* or *desthp*!). Because
these words — and especially *depths* — appear frequently in vocal
texts, their skillful articulation should be mastered.
    Do not omit the *th* in *months*. First, sing *mon-* with the tongue
outside of and touching the edges of the upper front teeth, the tongue
blade resting against the gum. Then whisper the first syllable of
thistle.
    Do not omit the *p* or the *th* in *depths*. Do not try to sing all

of the consonants simultaneously. They are likely to become reversed in the process. First sing *dep-* with an audibly explosive *p;* then protrude the tongue and draw it inward quickly while whispering the first syllable of *thistle.*

Practice singing:

months   depths

ARTICULATION OF THE VOICED ENDING: *-thes*

Because the ending *-the* (as in *breathe* or *scythe*) is voiced, any *s* added to it (as in *breathes* or *scythes* or *scythe's*) is voiced as a *z.* The combination of voiced *th* and *z* is difficult, but it is greatly facilitated by the tongue action we have described. Do not omit the *th.*
Practice singing:

breathes   (not *breeze*)
scythes   (not *size*)
bathes   (not *bays*)
sheathes   (not *she's*)
writhes   (not *ryes*)
loathes   (not *lows*)
wreathes   (not *wreaze*)

WORDS ENDING IN VOICELESS *th*, IN THE SINGULAR; IN VOICED *ths* IN THE PLURAL

A few words ending in voiceless *th* in the singular have voiced *ths* in the plural. The *s* is voiced as *z.* A common fault in the singing of these words is the omission of the *th,* changing the sense entirely. For example:

The *bahs* of spring (*baths*)
Like *maws* around a flame (*moths*)

Had I the *hen's* embroidered *claws*
        (*heaven's*)   (*cloths*)
            (*The Cloths of Heaven;* Yeats, Thomas Dunhill﹚
Below is a list of the words whose plural endings differ from the singular:

Voiceless	Voiced	
bath	baths	(*bathz*)
cloth	cloths	(*clothz*)
moth	moths	(*mothz*)
mouth	mouths	(*mouthz*)
oath	oaths	(*oathz*)
path	paths	(*pathz*)

Some words with voiceless *th* endings in the singular have either voiceless or voiced endings in the plural. These include: *youth, truth, sheath* (noun), and *wreath* (noun). Use whichever ending you find easier.

HOW TO CONNECT *th*
VOICELESS AND VOICED *th* BEFORE A VOWEL

When *th,* either voiceless or voiced, is followed by a syllable or word beginning with a vowel, use it as a connecting link, pronouncing it as the beginning of the next syllable or word. The *th* moves in this direction (➤).

Practice singing:

Voiceless		Voiced	
nothing	(*no-thing*)	father	(*fa-ther*)
mythical	(*my-thical*)	mother	(*mo-ther*)
pathos	(*pa-thos*)	brother	(*bro-ther*)
pathetic	(*pa-thetic*)	gather	(*ga-ther*)
strengthen	(*streng-then*)	feather	(*fea-ther*)
lengthen	(*leng-then*)	heather	(*hea-ther*)

my path is hard (*pa-this*)   breathe on (*brea-thon*)
the wrath of heaven (*wra-thof*)   smooth and still (*smoo-thand*)

Examples from vocal texts:

Thy king come*th* unto thee . . . He shall speak peace unto the hea*th*en . . . Why do the nations so furiously rage toge*th*er? . . . He that dwelle*th* in heaven.   (*Messiah*)

For I am not better than my fa*th*ers . . . I go my way in the streng*th* of the Lord.   (*Elijah*)

More I would, but dea*th* invades me.

Dea*th* is now a welcome guest.

(*Dido and Aeneas;* Tate, Purcell)

VOICELESS *th* BEFORE A CONSONANT AND BEFORE A PAUSE

When voiceless *th* occurs before a consonant, pronounce it as closely to the consonant as possible, with an explosion of air, but with no intervening vowel sound.

When voiceless *th* occurs before a pause, remember to blow an especially strong puff of air, but no vowel sound.

Practice singing:

death comes	- - after death.
earth smiles	- - upon the earth.
wrath vanishes	We suffer his wrath.

Examples from vocal texts:

For behold, darkness shall cover the ear*th*. (*Messiah*)

There is no brea*th* left in him . . . Yet have I spent my streng*th* for naught . . . Plenteous in mercy and tru*th* . . . (*Elijah*)

Present mir*th* ha*th* present laughter . . .

(*O Mistress Mine;* Shakespeare, Quilter)

Come away, come away, dea*th* . . .

Fly away, fly away, brea*th* . . .

(*Come Away, Death;* Shakespeare, Quilter)

VOICED *th* BEFORE A CONSONANT AND BEFORE A PAUSE

When voiced *th* occurs before a consonant or before a pause, do not draw in the tongue tip, but allow it to remain outside of the teeth while the *th* is being sounded. In this way, you will avoid the undesirable effect of an additional vowel sound.

Only in these two instances, which make an exception to the general rule, should the drawing inward of the tongue be omitted. Practice singing:

loathsome	In agony they writhe.
breathe deeply	- - while I breathe.
blithe carols	Their songs are blithe.
smooth voyage	He brandished a scythe.
bequeath to me	The deer came down to bathe.

But thou thereon didst only brea*the* . . .

(*Drink to Me Only with Thine Eyes;* Ben Jonson)

19. ADDITIONAL INSTRUCTIONS ABOUT *r*

In Spoken Dialogue — Before *oo* — In the Preposition *From*

We return briefly to *r*, the consonant that occupied three early sections of this manual. In practice, we have found it advisable to defer a few special instructions about *r* until the singer has had opportunity to master and make part of his equipment the general principles.

r IN SPOKEN DIALOGUE

This book is a manual for singers and is not intended to serve as a text for spoken English; but we include this one reference to dialogue because many a singer appears in stage works that call for talking as well as singing — and because *r* is a consonant that is influential in characterization of a role. The following two rules will enable the singer to maintain a plausible relationship between singing and speaking when he is cast in a work that involves both.

1. Use the American *r*.
2. Use the flipped *r* between vowels only, in two kinds of roles:
   a) Roles demanding dignity or elegance in characterization.
   b) Roles that require a British accent.

As illustration of a), let us examine Mozart's opera, *The Magic Flute*, which often is performed in English translation. In the spoken dialogue, Papageno, a colloquial fellow, uses only the American *r*; the aristocracy and other dignified characters, however, use the flipped *r* between vowels only, the American *r* otherwise. These characters include Tamino, a prince, Pamina, a princess, the Queen of the Night, her three ladies, Sarastro, a king, High Priests, etc. The arias, duets, and other fully accompanied parts of the opera are treated according to the directions for opera as outlined in Chapter 6, with a flipped *r* before every vowel (but not after *t* and *d*). Even when Papageno sings, he pronounces according to the rules for opera. He needs this stronger *r* in singing, to project over the orchestra. The audience is not aware of any difference between his pronunciation when sung and when spoken. It comes across to them when sung over the orchestra just as it sounds when spoken and unaccompanied.

As illustration of b), *The Beggar's Opera* by John Gay and the light operas of Gilbert and Sullivan are works that require a British accent.

DOUBLE *r* BEFORE *oo*

We have stressed the importance of flipping *r* only once. We have urged you not to roll or trill *r*. The importance of this fundamental principle in good English diction must be remembered at all times; and the one exception, which follows, is the only permissible exception, and is to be used only as an expedient in the specific condition indicated.

1. Pronounce two flips of the tongue for *r* before *oo*.

The vowel sound *oo*,* as in *too*, has so small a lip-rounding that it covers the sound of a preceding *r*. Therefore, when a flipped *r* is followed by the sound of *oo* (in a flipped *r* type of music), two flips of the tongue are necessary. Because of the small lip-rounding, only one flip will be heard, and the effect will seem entirely natural. Practice singing:

ruby	rumor
rude	ruthless
ruin	roof
rule	room
ruler	root

Examples in vocal texts:

Preach not me your musty *rules*. (*Air* from *Comus;* Milton, Arne)

Although thy breath be *rude* . . . (*Blow, Blow;* Shakespeare, Quilter)

I will make my kitchen, and you shall keep your *room* . . .
(*The Roadside Fire;* Stevenson, Vaughan Williams)

Do not heed their mild surprise —
Having passed the *Rubicon* . . .
(*Take a Pair of Sparkling Eyes*, from *The Gondoliers;* Gilbert and Sullivan)

---

*This vowel is discussed on page 136. Its phonetic symbol is [u].

2. Pronounce one flip of the tongue for *r* between a consonant and *oo*. This will be sufficient.

Practice singing:

brew	crude	groom
brute	frugal	prove
croon	fruit	proof
crucify	grew	prudent

Examples in vocal texts:

Haste then with ardor the bride*groom* to welcome.

(*Christmas Oratorio;* Bach)

The *fruit*-tree yielding *fruit* . . .

(*With Verdure Clad,* from *The Creation;* Haydn)

For love has more pow'r and less mercy than Fate

To make us seek *ruin,* and love those that hate.

(*I Attempt from Love's Sickness to Fly;* Howard, Purcell)

Where white flows the river and bright blows the *broom.*

(*The Roadside Fire;* Stevenson, Vaughan Williams)

3. Use the American *r,* as usual, after *t* or *d.* These consonants have such powers of projection that words with *tr* and *dr* need only the American *r,* even before *oo.*

Examples:

true	drew
truth	droop
intrude	druid

r IN THE PREPOSITION *from*

Do not flip the *r* in the word *from,* in any type of music, because the flipped *r* invariably lends a degree of emphasis, and *from* is a preposition which should not be stressed.

Use the American *r.*

20. *ng* [ŋ]

The sound that is spelled *ng* (as in the word *sing*) is a voiced consonant having no voiceless partner.

The spelling of this sound is misleading, because it has no relation to *n* or *g*. Observe that in the words *think* and *anxious*, the same sound, occurring before *k* and *x*, is spelled without *g*. The consonant *ng* as in *sing* is represented in the phonetic alphabet by the symbol [ŋ].

ARTICULATION OF *ng* [ŋ]

Raise the back of the tongue to meet the lowered soft palate, and add voice. The back of the tongue must be kept very relaxed, barely touching the soft palate, never pressing tightly against it; and the soft palate must be lowered only slightly. Otherwise, an unpleasantly nasal sound will result.

[ŋ] is always sung on the pitch of the preceding vowel, in this direction (◄—).
Practice singing:

sing	ring	long	bring
song	rang	strong	fling
sang	king	young	hang
sung	wing	thing	tongue
spring	swing	clang	among

HOW TO CONNECT *ng* [ŋ]

ng is sung on the pitch of the preceding vowel, moving in this direction (◄—), whether it is followed by a vowel or a consonant. There should be no vowel sound between *ng* and a following consonant.

Do not follow [ŋ] with the sound of hard *g*. It is true that there are a few words in which *ng* has the sound of [ŋ] plus hard *g*, but these words are exceptions, and will be discussed later in this chapter. All words ending in *ng*, and the vast majority of syllables

98

spelled with *ng* within a word, are pronounced [ŋ] without the sound of hard *g*.

Take great care to prevent the <u>unintentional</u> click of hard *g* after [ŋ]. Remember always that the back of the tongue must be relaxed and must touch the soft palate only lightly, while the soft palate is lowered only slightly. Then, after intoning the [ŋ], raise the soft palate gently, never abruptly, while the back of the tongue drops gently, never abruptly, to its normal position.

Practice singing:

singer	sing a song	sing to us
longing	long ago	long for
ringing	ring out	ring loud
wingèd	wing of a lark	wings
singing	king of glory	kingly
clingeth	fling away	fling back
springing	going up	going forth

ng [ŋ] BEFORE A PAUSE

There should be no vowel sound after [ŋ] when it occurs before a pause. Stop the tone before the soft palate and tongue separate. Practice singing:

The birds sang.
Our hearts were young.
We hail our noble king.

Further examples:

I'll give you back your letters,
I'll give you back your ri*ng*,
But I'll ne'er forget my own true love
As lo*ng* as so*ng*-birds si*ng*.
       (*Go 'Way from My Window;* John Jacob Niles)
Orpheus with his lute made trees
And the mountain tops that freeze
Bow themselves when he did si*ng:*
To his music plants and flowers
Ever spru*ng;* as sun and showers
There had made a lasti*ng* spri*ng*.
       (*Orpheus with His Lute;* Shakespeare, William Schuman)

WHEN TO PRONOUNCE A HARD *g* IN *ng*
[ŋg]

There are only a few words in which *ng* has the sound of *ng* plus hard *g* (which is *g* as in *go*). (The phonetic symbols for this combination are [ŋg].) These words may be summarized in the following three divisions:

1. In the comparative and superlative of *long, strong*, and *young*.

No Hard *g*	*ng* Plus Hard *g*	*ng* Plus Hard *g*
long	longer *(long-ger)*	longest *(long-gest)*
strong	stronger *(strong-ger)*	strongest *(strong-gest)*
young	younger *(young-ger)*	youngest *(young-gest)*

2. In the words *elongate* and *prolongate*, with their various endings. (Pronounced *elong-gate* and *prolong-gate*.)

3. (a) When the first syllable of a word has a meaning totally different from the meaning of the complete word.

   (b) When the first syllable of a word has no meaning by itself.

Examples of (a):

First Syllable No Hard *g*	Meaning of Complete Word Totally Different	Pronunciation *ng* Plus Hard *g*
sing	single	*sing-gle*
hung	hunger	*hung-ger*
tang	tangle	*tang-gle*
bang	bangle	*bang-gle*

Examples of (b):

First Syllable Having No Meaning by Itself	Complete Word	Pronunciation *ng* Plus Hard *g*
fing-	finger	*fing-ger*
ling-	linger	*ling-ger*
ang-	anger	*ang-ger*

Additional examples of (b):

jangle	angle	mingle	languish
jingle	anguish	English	languor
jungle	tingle	language	languid

Exception: *gingham* has no hard *g*.

NOTE on Ending: *-nge*

The ending *-nge* (as in *change*) has the sound of *n* plus "soft" *g*.

21. *h*

h is a voiceless consonant having no voiced partner.

ARTICULATION OF *h*

With the mouth open, blow a stream of air strong enough to be clearly audible.

Do not fear a failure of breath. (See page 30.)

h is a consonant that often suffers from neglect. Yet *h* adds to the expressiveness of many words, because it gives the effect of a sigh, which can be either pleasurable (as in *happy, heaven, hope,* etc.) or ominous (as in *heavy, hunger, horror, hate,* etc.).

Practice singing:

happy	heavy	hurry
heaven	hunger	hasten
hope	horror	he
haven	hate	her
home	haunted	perhaps
heal	hopeless	house
help	hounded	behead
holy	harm	hand

*H*ear Ye, Israel; *h*ear what the Lord speaketh: "Oh, *h*adst thou *h*eeded my commandments." . . . and *h*is *H*oly One, to *h*im oppressed by Tyrants . . . I am *H*e that comforteth . . . Say, w*h*o art thou . . . w*h*o *h*ath stretched forth the *h*eavens . . .

(*Elijah;* Mendelssohn)

All is *h*ealed, all is *h*ealth.
*H*igh summer *h*olds the earth.
*H*earts all w*h*ole.

(*Sure on This Shining Night;* Agee, Barber)

Oh, they'll *h*ang me, they'll *h*ang me . . .
That comes of being *h*anged so *h*igh
On the top of *H*angin' *H*ill.

(*The Gambler's Lament;* John Jacob Niles)

In a number of words, *h* is a silent letter, appearing in the spelling, but not in the pronunciation.

For example:

honest	exhaust
honor	exhortation
hour	rhyme
heir	forehead (*fah-red*)*

**fah-red is the preferred pronunciation, although fore-head is sometimes given.

22. *wh* AND *w*

wh (voiceless) and *w* (voiced) constitute a pair of consonants articulated through protruded, rounded, almost closed lips.

In studying these consonants, we shall start with the voiced member of the pair, *w*, because the articulation of *wh* may be presented more concisely after an examination of *w*.

INITIAL *w* IS A CONSONANT; FINAL *w* IS A VOWEL

w is a consonant at the beginning of a syllable (*wind, twist, always, forward*). When it occurs at the end of a syllable, it is a vowel (*now, law, awful*), and, as such, will be discussed in the second part of this manual.

ARTICULATION OF THE CONSONANT *w*

With protruded, rounded lips, narrowed at the sides, and opened only slightly, sound the voice. The result resembles the vowel sound *oo*, as in *too*.

You may wonder why initial *w* is considered a consonant and not a vowel. It is so considered because in speech, the lips start in the *oo* position, but widen immediately with a definite thrust to introduce the vowel that follows the *w*. This vigorous widening of the lips gives *w* its consonantal quality.

In singing, which is more sustained than speech, an effective means of emphasis for an important word beginning with *w* is the prolongation of the *oo* sound.
Practice singing:

wise	(*oo-ise*)	wake	(*oo-ake*)	weep	(*oo-eep*)
wonder	(*oo-under*)	weary	(*oo-eary*)	woe	(*oo-oe*)
watch	(*oo-atch*)	waiting	(*oo-aiting*)	wail	(*oo-ail*)

When the consonant *w* is preceded by a word or syllable ending in a vowel sound (*they watch* or *bewail*), sing the *oo* on the pitch of that preceding vowel sound, in this direction (◀). Sing *theyoo-atch* or *beoo-ail*. In these circumstances, however, never carry the *oo* sound from one pitch to the other, because such a

103

swoop will bring about one of the most objectionable devices in singing — a scoop.

Practice singing the following phrases and words, sounding the two vowels on two different pitches, and intoning the *oo* on the pitch of the first vowel (which of course does not change):

they watch   (*theyoo-atch*)   bewail   (*beoo-ail*)
he wakes   (*heoo-akes*)   await   (*aoo-ait*)
I wonder as *I wander* (*Ioo-onder as Ioo-ander*)

(John Jacob Niles)

Prepare ye *the way* of the Lord (*theoo-ay*)   (*Messiah*)
The voice of *the winter* (*theoo-inter*)

(*Sleep Now;* Joyce, Barber)

Remember that *r* is omitted before a consonant. Therefore the consonant *w*, when preceded by *r*, is sung on the pitch of the vowel before the printed but silent *r*.
Practice singing:

summer winds   (*summe'oo-inds*)
you are wise   (*you ah-oo-ise*)

When the consonant *w* is preceded by one of the consonants that moves in this direction (◄—) (*m, n,* final *l,* and *ng*), the *oo* sound also moves in this direction (◄—); it is sung on the pitch of the preceding consonant.
Practice singing:

calm waters (*calmoo-aters*)   cool winds   (*cooloo-inds*)
even ways   (*evenoo-ays*)   keeping watch (*keepingoo-atch*)

When the consonant *w* is preceded by a word ending in one of the consonants that moves in this direction (—►), the *oo* sound also moves in this direction (—►); it is sung on the pitch of the word beginning with *w*. In cases like this, the preceding consonant actually starts the *w* word. For example: *red wine* is sung as *re-dooine*.
Practice singing:

red wine   (*re-dooine*)   like wings (*li-kooings*)
in great want (*grea-tooant*)   south wind (*sou-thooind*)

SILENT *w*

The above instructions are, of course, not to be applied to words in which *w* is spelled but not pronounced. In *write, wrong, wrath, writhe,* etc., the function of *w* is purely visual.

wh

wh is the voiceless sound corresponding to *w* which is voiced.

wh is represented in the phonetic alphabet by the symbol [hw]. We mention this because it is helpful in illustrating the actual sound of this consonant. It is interesting to note that in early English, words now spelled with *wh* were spelled with *hw* (*hwen, hwat,* etc.).

ARTICULATION OF *wh*

Although *wh* and *w* start with the same lip position, the treatment of *wh* differs sharply from that of *w*. There is no *oo* sound in *wh*.

Protrude and round the lips, narrowing them at the sides and holding them only slightly open, just as for *w;* but in place of sounding *oo,* blow a strong *h*. While aspirating the *h,* widen the lips abruptly to pronounce whatever vowel sound follows the *wh*.

The *w* in *wh* does not represent a sound; it merely indicates the shape of the lips. For example, the word *when* has only one vowel sound: *e*. It would be entirely incorrect to pronounce it *hoo-en*.

As a preliminary exercise, whisper the word *whip,* imitating the sound of a whip being flicked through the air. Then whisper the word *whisper*.

Practice singing:

whip	(not *wip,*	not *hoo-ip*)
whisper	(not *wisper,*	not *hoo-isper*)
which	(not *witch,*	not *hoo-itch*)
while	(not *wile,*	not *hoo-ile*)
when	(not *wen,*	not *hoo-en*)
where	(not *wear,*	not *hoo-ere*)
whether	(not *weather,*	not *hoo-ether*)
what	(not *watt,*	not *hoo-at*)
why	(not *wy,*	not *hoo-eye*)

who   In this word, the *w* has no real function. It is pronounced merely *hoo* with no whip of the lips.

Many people indulge in the curious habit not only of omitting the *h* of *wh,* but also of inserting an *h* where there is only a plain *w*. This vagary changes *whether* to *weather,* and, conversely, *weather* into *whether*. A mournful *whine* acquires an unexpected alcoholic content as a mournful *wine,* and a good *wine* is adulterated into a good *whine. Which* is *witch,* and *witch* is *which* . . . and these few examples may serve as a reminder always to sing *w* and *wh* accurately.

Examples of *w* and *wh* from vocal texts:

> And the *wh*eel's kick and the *w*ind's song and the *wh*ite sail's shaking . . .
>
> To the gull's *w*ay and the *wh*ale's *w*ay *wh*ere the *w*ind's like a *wh*etted knife . . .
>
> > (*Sea Fever;* Masefield, Ireland)
>
> Sandalwood, cedar*w*ood, and s*w*eet *wh*ite *w*ine.
>
> > (*Cargoes;* Masefield, Dobson)
>
> *Wh*ence they come and *wh*ither they go
>
> *W*e often *w*onder but never know . . . (*Clouds;* anon., Charles)

23. *s* AND *z*

s and *z* constitute a pair of consonants articulated by identical tongue positions. They differ only in that *s*, being voiceless, is aspirated, whereas *z* is voiced.

The sound *s* is spelled *s* (as in *some*) and *c* (as in *ice*). It is represented in the phonetic alphabet by the symbol [s].

The sound *z* is spelled *z* (as in *lazy*) and *s* (as in *his*). It is represented in the phonetic alphabet by the symbol [z].

Because *s* and *z* present no particular problems in singing, except to people who lisp, we have placed the directions for the articulation of *s* and *z* in our next chapter, which is devoted to the overcoming of a lisp.

How to Connect *s* or *z*

s or *z* before a vowel

When either *s* or *z* is followed by a syllable or word beginning with a vowel sound, use the *s* or *z* as a connecting link, pronouncing it at the beginning of the next syllable or word, in this direction (➤). *z* takes the pitch of the following vowel.
Practice singing:

loosen	(*loo-sen*)	wiser	(*wi-zer*)
rejoicing	(*re-joi-cing*)	lazy	(*la-zy*)
miss it	(*mi-sit*)	his own	(*hi-zown*)
cross over	(*cro-sover*)	it is enough	(*i-ti-zen-ough*)

s or *z* before a consonant

s or *z*, followed by a consonant, should be pronounced immediately before the consonant with no intervening vowel sound.
Practice singing:

useful	(*u-sful*)	wisdom	(*wi-zdom*)
mystery	(*my-stery*)	rosebud	(*ro-zbud*)
voiceless	(*voi-sless*)	puzzling	(*pu-zling*)
kiss me	(*ki-sme*)	his name	(*hi-zname*)
less than	(*le-sthan*)	the breeze blew	(*bree-zblew*)
moss green	(*mo-sgreen*)	in days gone by	(*day-zgone by*)

107

s BEFORE *s*
AND
z BEFORE *z*

When a word ending in *s* is followed by a word beginning with *s*, and when a word ending in *z* is followed by a word beginning with *z*, prolong the *s* or the *z*, making no separation between the words.

Practice singing:

less sweet	(*lessweet*)	his zeal	(*hizzeal*)
her voice sings	(*voissings*)	has zest	(*hazzest*)
her lips speak	(*lipsspeak*)	spring's zephyr	(*springzzephyr*)

z BEFORE *s*
AND
s BEFORE *z*

When a word ending in *z* is followed by a word beginning with *s*, and when a word ending in *s* is followed by a word beginning with *z*, there is no need to separate the two consonants. Merge one into the other.

Practice singing:

his soul	(*hizsoul*)	he lacks zeal	(*lackszeal*)
the trees sway	(*treezsway*)	life's zest	(*lifeszest*)

s OR *z* BEFORE A PAUSE

When *s* or *z* occurs before a pause, there should be no additional vowel sound. Stop the tone before removing the tongue from the *s* or *z* position.

The voicing of final *z* must be maintained firmly to its conclusion. If the voicing is not maintained, the sound will wind up in an *s*, so that, for example, *eyes* will seem to be *ice*. It is a fact that the listener's impression of this sound is what he hears at its termination.

Practice singing:

your shining eyes	(not *ice*)	hear my sighs
my greatest prize	(not *price*)	under the trees
who in slumber lies	(not *Pediculi!*)	of former days

24. *s* AND *z* FOR THOSE WHO LISP

LISPING

One of the most common defects arising from difficulty with *s* and *z* is a lisp. "Lisp," for practical purposes, is a generic word to indicate degradation of *s* and *z* into various distortions.

CAUSES OF LISPING

Any of the following procedures may be responsible for a lisp:

sides of tongue not held against upper side teeth (causing lateral escape of air);

tongue tip not held in center (causing lateral escape of air);

crooked lips (causing lateral escape of air);

tongue tip touching upper gum;

tongue tip touching teeth (this results in a *th* sound);

tongue tip too far back (this brings about an *sh* sound);

tongue tip against lower gum or teeth (this brings about an *sh* sound);

too forceful explosion of air.

A fundamental remedy for lisping is the proper articulation of *s* and *z*, as in the following instructions. A special section of remedial drills is also included in this chapter.

CORRECT ARTICULATION OF *s* AND *z*

1. Hold the sides of the tongue firmly against the edges of the upper side teeth so that no air can escape laterally.

2. Groove the center of the tongue.

3. Point the tip of the tongue toward the exact center of the upper front teeth.

4. Place the tip of the tongue very close to the upper front teeth. Do not allow the tongue tip to touch the front teeth or the gum.

5. Keep the lips symmetrical. Do not pull one or both to the sides of the face.

6. (a) For *s*, aspirate by blowing a slight stream of air, directing

it against the upper front teeth.

> Do not blow too forcibly.

> (b) For *z*, add voice in place of aspiration, singing the consonant on a pitch.

Although careful observance of the above rules will remedy a lisp, it is usually necessary to employ special exercises when the lisp has long been a characteristic of the singer's articulation, and the following suggestions are recommended for careful practice by singers who are troubled with a chronic lisp.

CAUTION

Practice of the *s* and *z* drills should be limited to ten or fifteen minute sessions. Several short practice periods daily are preferable to one long one. Continued repetition of tongue exercises, without intervals of rest, will fatigue the tongue muscles and cause blurring of *s* and *z*.

DRILLS FOR *s* TO AID IN OVERCOMING A LISP

Keep the tongue in the position described in the first two directions for articulation of *s* and, with the lips symmetrical in shape, say:

> *tsoo, tsoo, tsoo, tsoo*

The purpose of this exercise is simple. When your tongue tip moves from *t* to *s*, in saying *tsoo*, it draws away from the gum and automatically finds the right position for a clear *s*.

Now say: *tsoo, soo, tsoo, soo,* and each time you say *soo* by itself, place your tongue tip in the same position it occupied when *soo* was part of *tsoo*.

As a helpful corrective exercise, we advise that you pronounce the *s* in a thin, shrill sound similar to the whistle of a peanut vendor's stand. This should be done intentionally only in practicing the drills. When you encounter *s* in actual singing or speaking, this exaggeration will automatically be modified.

Practice very slowly, listening carefully to each sound:

tsoon - soon	*tsahm* - psalm	*tso* - so
tsoot - soot	*tsat* - sat	*tsouth* - south
tsaw - saw	*tset* - set	*tsoil* - soil
tsup - sup	*tsit* - sit	*tsigh* - sigh
tsir - sir	*tsee* - see	*tsay* - say

There are some who find it more helpful to practice *ns* (as in *manse*) than *ts*. Experiment with the following to determine which is better for you:

Keep the tongue in the position described in the first two directions for articulation of *s* and, with the lips symmetrical in shape, say:

   nsoo, nsoo, nsoo, nsoo

Now say: *nsoo, soo, nsoo, soo,* and each time you say *soo* by itself, place your tongue tip in the same position it occupied when *soo* was part of *nsoo*.

If this has proved to be more helpful than *tsoo*, practice very slowly, listening to each sound:

nsoon - soon	*nsahm* - psalm	*nso* - so
nsoot - soot	*nsat* - sat	*nsouth* - south
nsaw - saw	*nset* - set	*nsoil* - soil
nsup - sup	*nsit* - sit	*nsigh* - sigh
nsir - sir	*nsee* - see	*nsay* - say

Next, practice the following list of words in which *s* appears before and after various vowels in a variety of situations. A l w a y s . . . p r a c t i c e . . . s l o w l y. This direction is stressed, however irritatingly repetitious it may seem, because these exercises will be ineffective if they are done superficially or hurriedly. First, practice the words in the left-hand column, reading downward; then practice each line reading across:

bassoon	loosen	loose	roost	stoop	strew
forsook	pussy	puss		stood	
assault	mossy	moss	*tossed	store	straw
asunder	fussing	fuss	dust	stumble	struck
usurp	adversity	verse	first	stir	
massage	parcel	parse	past	star	
dissatisfy	massive	mass	hast	stab	strap
assemble	lesson	less	best	step	strength
rescind	whisper	miss	*kissed	stick	stricken
receive	peaceable	peace	feast	steed	street
disown	closer	dose	most	stone	stroke
	dousing	douse	*doused	stout	
assoil	rejoicing	rejoice	*rejoiced		destroy
Messiah	icy	ice	*iced	sty	strike
assail	racing	ace	waste	stay	stray

---

*Remember that the suffix *-ed* is pronounced as *t* when it follows a voiceless consonant.

Now, practice *s:*
    in combination with various other consonants;
    in words that include more than one *s* sound.
B e . . . s u r e . . . t o . . . p r a c t i c e . . . s l o w l y .

slew	dukes	proofs	assist	restless
slaughter	walks	coughs	cease	restlessness
slumber	ducks	puffs	ceased	*expectancy
slur	works	turfs	ceaseless	solace
slash	lacks	laughs	*express	surcease
slept	wrecks	chefs	*expressed	success
sleep	weeks	griefs	mistrust	suspect
slow	yokes	loafs	since	sustain
slight	likes	life's	sets	suppress
slay	lakes	waifs	sister	system
slot	locks	scoffs	mistress	listless

DRILLS FOR z TO AID IN OVERCOMING A LISP

Keep the tongue in the position described in the first two directions for articulation of *s* and *z* (page 109). Add voice, instead of blowing air. With the lips symmetrical in shape, say:

dzoo, dzoo, dzoo, dzoo

Then, say: *dzoo, zoo, dzoo, zoo*
Or, if it is more helpful in your case, say:

nzoo, nzoo, nzoo, nzoo;   then, *nzoo, zoo, nzoo, zoo*

Practice slowly either the first or second double column below. (Most of the letter combinations are merely sounds to be incorporated presently into words):

dzoo - zoo	*nzoo* - zoo
dzaw - zaw	*nzaw* - zaw
dzuh - zuh	*nzuh* - zuh
dzest - zest	*nzest* - zest
dzip - zip	*nzip* - zip
dzeal - zeal	*nzeal* - zeal
dzone - zone	*nzone* - zone
dzah - zah	*nzah* - zah
dzigh - zigh	*nzigh* - zigh
dzay - zay	*nzay* - zay

---

*This *x* is actually [ks].

Now, practice the words in the left-hand column, reading downward. Then practice each line reading across:

resume	user	use	*used
resort	pausing	pause	paused
result	dozen	does	
resemble	pleasant	says	
resilient	lizard	his	fizzed
	pleasing	agrees	teased
ozone	posing	rose	closed
resound	rousing	allows	aroused
	poison	poise	poised
**exact	dazzle	has	jazzed
desire	wiser	eyes	advised
azalea	lazy	days	gazed
deserve	jersey	hers	

Next, practice *z* in combination with various other consonants:

webs	calls	lives
odes	homes	loves
ends	tones	leaves
begs	longs	breathes

Practice the following words which have both *s* and *z:*

seize	resist	exist	exhaust
possess	sobs	surprised	sighs
sizzle	sings	exasperate	soothes

Examples of *s* and *z* in song texts:

Cease, O my sad soul, cease to mourn.
I see my love and faith are paid
With nothing but disdain and scorn.
> (*Cease, O My Sad Soul;* Purcell)

The poor soul sat sighing by a sycamore tree.
> (*Willow Song;* Shakespeare, Music — Time of Elizabeth)

The place is‿sealed
An unclaimed sovereignty of voiceless‿song,
And all th'unravished silence
Belong to some sweet singer lost or unrevealed.
So is my soul become a silent place.
Oh, may I awake from this uneasy night.

---

*Remember that the suffix *-ed* is pronounced as *d* after a voiced consonant.
**The *x* in *exact* is actually [gz].

To find some voice of music manifold.
Let it be shape of sorrow with wan face,
Or love that swoons on sleep, or else delight
That is as wide-eyed as a marigold.

(*The Green River;* Douglas, Carpenter)

I've snuff and tobaccy, and excellent jacky,
I've scissors, and watches, and knives;
I've ribbons and laces to set off the faces
Of pretty young sweethearts and wives.

(*H.M.S. Pinafore;* Gilbert and Sullivan)

For further practice of *s* and *z* in song texts, we recommend study of the following material:

Once a Lady Was Here; Bowles
Sea Fever; Masefield, Ireland
Sea-Shell; Lowell, Engel

25. *sh* AND [ʒ]

The voiceless sound *sh*, as in *she*, and the voiced sound of *s* as in *vision*, constitute a pair of consonants articulated by an identical tongue position.

The sound *sh* is represented in the phonetic alphabet by the symbol [ʃ].

The phonetic symbol [ʒ] represents the sound spelled by *s* in *vision* and by *z* in *azure*, and as such it appears medially, that is between the vowel sounds within a word. It is also spelled by *g* in a few words borrowed from the French, such as *mirage*. In these few words only, it appears as a final consonant. There is no specific spelling in English for the sound [ʒ], and all of us should be grateful for the existence of the phonetic symbol as a convenience in making notations on copies of vocal music or writing books on diction.

ARTICULATION OF *sh* AND [ʒ]

Place the sides of the tongue firmly against the edges of the upper side teeth, and point the tongue tip toward the center of the upper front teeth. Hold the tongue tip farther back from the teeth than for *s* (as in *see*) or *z* (as in *zoo*).

Blow a strong stream of air for *sh*. This consonant is easily articulated and easily heard.

There is no blowing of air for [ʒ]. In place of the aspirate sound, add voice.

Examples:

sh			[ʒ]	
she	sure	ancient	vision	azure
shine	crash	ocean	pleasure	mirage
shame	fresh	motion	measure	rouge

*S*ure on this *sh*ining night
Of star-made *sh*adows round . . .
(Sure on This Shining Night; Agee, Barber)

115

How to Connect *sh* and [ʒ]

sh and [ʒ] before a syllable or word beginning with a vowel are pronounced as the start of the next syllable or word, moving in this direction (➤).

Examples:

crashing	(*cra-shing*)	vision	(*vi-sion*)
ancient	(*an-shent*)	azure	(*a-zure*)
flash of	(*fla-shof*)	mirage appears	(*mira-geappears*)

There should be no vowel sound after *sh* or [ʒ] when it appears before a syllable or word beginning with a consonant, or before a pause.

Examples:

rush forth (*ru-shforth*)   mirage vanished (*mira-ʒvanished*)
— on the lonely marsh.   — it was a mirage.

FINAL *sh* BEFORE A WORD BEGINNING WITH *sh*

When a word ending in *sh* is followed by a word beginning with *sh*, the two words should not be disconnected. Sing one long *sh*.

Examples:

fresh‿showers
blush‿shyly
And all *flesh‿shall* see it together.   (*Messiah*)

26. *ch* AND "SOFT" *g* OR *j*

ch, as in *choose*, and "soft" *g*, as in *George*, constitute a pair of consonants articulated by means of the tongue tip and gum. *ch* is voiceless and soft *g* is voiced. The voiced sound is also spelled *j*, as in *joy*.

ARTICULATION OF *ch*

To articulate *ch*, as in *choose*, place the sides of the tongue firmly against the upper side teeth, with the tongue tip touching the center of the upper gum. Blow a vigorous puff of air and instantly lower the tongue tip to the *sh* position. This sound is actually *tsh*, and is represented in the phonetic alphabet by the symbols [tʃ].

The *t* and *sh* are not separated, but are pronounced as a unit: as a *sh* which starts with the tongue tip touching the gum. The puff of air is uninterrupted.

This sound is easily projected and is an expressive component of many words.

Examples:

charm	chill	touch
cheer	chase	watch
cherish	choose	search

sh AND *ch* MUST NOT BE INTERCHANGED

Do not sing *shoes* for *choose*.

Do not sing *share* for *chair*.

Do not sing *sheer* for *cheer*.

Do not sing *mush* for *much*. ("I love him so *mush*")

Do not sing *wash* for *watch*. ("I have *washed* all night")

ARTICULATION OF SOFT *g* OR *j*

To articulate soft *g*, as in *George*, or *j*, as in *joy*, use the same tongue position and action as for *ch*, but add voice instead of blowing a puff of air. This sound is actually *d* plus [ʒ] as in *vision*, and is represented in the phonetic alphabet by the symbols [dʒ].

The *d* and [ʒ] are not separated, but are pronounced as a unit, as a [ʒ] that starts with the tongue tip touching the gum. The voicing is uninterrupted.

Examples:

gem	joy
age	joke
edge	join
urge	judge

ch MUST NOT BE SUBSTITUTED FOR SOFT *g* OR *j*

Some singers, in a violent effort to insure distinctness, over-emphasize soft *g* or *j* by blowing a puff of air instead of voicing it. This brings about the substitution of *ch* for the voiced sound — a ludicrous and often misleading effect.

Do not sing *chentle* for *gentle*.

Do not sing *chem* for *gem*.

Do not sing *chump* for *jump*.

Do not sing *chewel* for *jewel*.

Do not sing *chuch* for *judge*.

Do not sing *cheer* for *jeer*. (". . . deriding him with taunts and *cheers*")

Do not sing *choke* for *joke*. ("I am only *choking*.")

HOW TO CONNECT *ch* AND SOFT *g* OR *j*

ch and soft *g* or *j* before a syllable or word beginning with a vowel are pronounced as the start of the following syllable or word, moving in this direction (→).

Examples:

reaching	(*rea-ching*)	magic	(*ma-gic*)
which is	(*whi-chis*)	the age of reason	(*a-geof*)

Ri*ch* and rare were the gems she wore. (*ri-chand*)

(Irish Folk Song)

From the rage of the tempest . . . (*ra-geof*)

Here in this deathlike region . . . (*re-gion*)

(*Hear Me, Ye Winds and Waves;* Handel)

When *ch* appears before a syllable or word beginning with a consonant, or before a pause, there is a strong puff of air, but no additional vowel sound. When soft *g* appears in the same situation, it is voiced, without a puff of air; and here, too, there is no additional vowel sound.

Practice singing:

teach them	(*tea-chthem*)	Judge me not.	(*ju-dgme*)
watch for me	(*wa-tchfor*)	Begrudge them not.	(*Begru-dgthem*)
Lift the latch.		Beware his rage.	

A NOTE ON *righteous*

The medial consonant in the word *righteous* is *ch* [tʃ].

FINAL *ch* FOLLOWED BY *ch*

SOFT *g* OR *j* FOLLOWED BY SOFT *g* OR *j*

When a word ending in *ch* is followed by a word beginning with *ch,* each *ch* must be sounded.

Examples:

each child	(*eachchild*)
rich choice	(*richchoice*)

Similarly, when a word ending in soft *g* or *j* is followed by a word beginning with soft *g* or *j,* both consonants are necessary.

Examples:

We urge justice	(*urgejustice*)
A huge joke	(*hugejoke*)

There must be no vowel sound between the repeated consonants.

27. SUMMARY OF CONNECTIONS

Now that all consonants have been discussed, it will be helpful to have a summary of connections.

Consonants moving in this direction (←):

$\left. \begin{array}{l} m \\ n \end{array} \right\}$ When preceded by a vowel.

ng

Consonants moving in either direction (←) or (→):

 v Between vowels on different pitches, (←) or (→) whichever is lower.

  In other situations when preceded by a vowel (←).

 l Initial l (→)

  Final l (←)

 w Moves with whatever precedes it (←) or (→).

All other consonants move in this direction (→).

28. SUMMARY OF SPECIAL DIRECTIONS FOR INCIDENTAL WORDS

In discussing the consonants, special directions have been included for de-emphasizing prepositions and other incidental words, so that stiltedness might be avoided. These consonantal directions are summarized herewith. The vowels will be discussed in Chapter 42.

at	Sound only one *t* when the next word begins with *t*.
to	Sound only one *t* when the preceding word ends in *t*.
of	Do not emphasize the *v*.
	Exception: *of you.*
and	Do not emphasize the *d* by adding a vowel sound.
the	Do not emphasize the *th.*
with	Voice the *th.* When followed by a word beginning with *th,* sound only the second *th.*
from	Use the American *r* in every type of music.

Part II
29. VOWELS; PHONETIC ALPHABET

For clarity of diction, vowels have as much importance as consonants. A singer who distorts vowel sounds is garbling the words, even though his articulation of consonants may be admirable. However expertly he produces his consonants, when he sings *feet* for *fate*, *leave* for *live*, *vice* for *voice*, he confuses the audience. Vowels must be sung accurately.

Discussion of vowels prompts a restatement of the fact that this book is not a treatise on tone production. It is a treatise on word production — and these two forms of production supplement each other. Some of the suggestions for intelligible articulation of vowels have proved to be helpful to many singers in achieving good tone; but they still are to be regarded as accessories to vocal technique rather than a vocal method in themselves.

The most important guide to the pronunciation of vowels is the ear; to hear a vowel sound correctly is the essential factor in its production. Although the function of the tongue was discussed in the study of consonants, there will be little allusion to it as we proceed with vowels. We have found, in our experience with hundreds of singers, that most English-speaking vocalists make the tongue adjustments for various English vowels automatically, and that stress on this subject in a diction manual for singers is not pertinent. Where a singer encounters serious difficulties in the use of the tongue as part of his vocal apparatus, it is advisable for him to work this out with his voice teacher as an element in his general tone production. There will be occasional mention of the shape of the lips in the pronunciation of certain vowels, but these references will be few because there are only a few vowels whose proper articulation involves the lips.

ABOUT THE PHONETIC ALPHABET

In our study of vowels, it will be a convenience to make use of the symbols of the phonetic alphabet. The reason for this will be made evident by the following illustrations. In the sentence *Many a baby has a tall father,* there are six pronunciations of the letter *a.* Therefore we cannot speak of the "sound of *a*" because no one would know which sound we had in mind. In the sentence "With *each breath,* my *yearning heart bears great fear,*" we find seven pronunciations of *ea.* It would be cumbersome to be obliged to say "as in," every time we wished to designate a sound. Comment on diphthongs, which are composed of two sounds in one syllable, would always necessitate a double "as in." The phonetic alphabet is a device in which each sound is represented by a symbol, regardless of the spelling. There is no need to memorize all of the symbols, although we shall present the complete list for reference; later, we shall designate seven symbols to be memorized for a specific purpose — the study of diphthongs.

The symbols used are a part of the International Phonetic Alphabet, devised in Continental Europe. Any singers who have been aided by this alphabet in their study of French or German, for example, will find it a valuable basis for comparison with English; for any English sound that also appears in these languages is represented by the same symbol.

PHONETIC ALPHABET

Vowels

Symbol	Key Word	Symbols	Key Word
		Diphthongs	
[ɑ]	father (*ah*)	[ɑɪ]	night
[ɛ]	wed	[ɛɪ]	day
[ɪ]	it	[ɔɪ]	boy
[i]	me	[ɑu]	now
[æ]	cat	[ou]	no
[u]	too	[ɛə]	air
[ʊ]	full	[ɪə]	ear
[o]	*o*bey (unstressed)	[ɔə]	ore
[ɔ]	warm	[ʊə]	sure
[з]	learn		**Triphthongs**
[ʌ]	up	[ɑɪə]	ire
[ə]	sof*a* (unstressed; neutral vowel)	[ɑʊə]	our

For the sake of completeness, we add below three symbols for sounds used in spoken English, but not in English singing:

[a]   ask (as sometimes spoken)
[ɒ]   hot (as sometimes spoken)
[e]   ate

CONSONANTS

The majority of consonants have symbols that are identical with the letters used in spelling: b,d,f,g,h,k,l,m,n,p,r,s,t,v,w,z.

Symbol	Key Word	Symbol	Key Word
[ŋ]	si*ng*	[ʃ]	*sh*e
[θ]	*th*in	[tʃ]	*ch*oose
[ð]	*th*ine	[ʒ]	vi*s*ion
[hw]	*wh*en	[dʒ]	George ("soft" *g*) / *j*oy
[j]	*y*ou		

30. [ɑ] AS IN FATHER
WE CALL IT *AH*

The phonetic symbol [ɑ] represents the vowel sound in the word *father,* and in such words as *star, heart, calm.* This sound is basic to singing; it is the theme of which many other vowels are variations. It sometimes is called "the Italian *ah*" because it is the equivalent of the sound indicated in Italian by the letter *a.* The term *ah* is, in fact, so familiar to singers as a designation of this sound, that we shall use it extensively in this manual. We shall employ the phonetic symbol [ɑ] only in a few instances where it will be more convenient than *ah.*

It would be outside the scope of this manual to discuss the internal mechanics involved in the production of *ah.* The voice teacher may, in the course of his instruction, explain the physiological details to the singer. Perhaps the singer may hear about the process from a laryngologist who describes what happens when his patient says "ah" to "open the throat" for examination.

One physical aspect is, however, well within our diction territory — the relaxation of the lips. And it is simply relaxation, with no specifications as to the shape that the lips must assume. All that the singer is asked to do is to permit his lips to open comfortably. There must be no feeling of tenseness in the lips. There must be no awareness of the lips at all.

Special caution: Do not protrude the lips. The result would be [ɔ] as in *warm,* a vowel much darker than *ah.* Many singers inadvertently substitute [ɔ] for *ah* because they protrude the lips. They sing *store* for *star, port* for *part,* "hort" for *heart, pork* for *park,* etc. Practice singing:

father	heart	park	arm	*calm
star	start	lark	charm	*palm
far	farmer	dark	alarm	*psalm
part	martyr	embark	garden	*qualm

---

*The *l* is silent.

125

Examples in vocal texts:

In sweet music is such *a*rt
Killing care and grief of he*a*rt . . .

(*Orpheus with His Lute;* Shakespeare, William Schuman)

Refrain, audacious t*a*r . . .
Remember what you *a*re.

(*H.M.S. Pinafore;* Gilbert and Sullivan)

I weep for wonder w*a*nd'ring f*a*r alone
Of shadows on the st*a*rs.

(*Sure on This Shining Night;* Agee, Barber)

31. [ɛ] AS IN WED

The phonetic symbol [ɛ] represents the vowel sound in the word *wed*. Examples of other spellings: *head, friend, guest, bury, any, said, says, leopard.*

Many singers indulge in needless torture when they sing this vowel. Some tense the lower lip; some tighten the lower jaw; some squeeze the corners of the mouth. All such efforts belong in the department of useless strains. Merely drop the lower lip. When we do this, the jaw drops with it. Do not push the jaw down; do not force the jaw into a wide or tense or excessively low position; do not think of the jaw at all. Simply let the lower lip drop comfortably and easily, in a relaxed manner.

SPECIAL NOTE ABOUT *Any* AND *Many*

Regional speech habits cause some singers to mispronounce *any* and *many*. These words should be [ɛnɪ] and [mɛnɪ]; never [ɪnɪ] and [mɪnɪ].

DEVICE FOR HIGH NOTES

When [ɛ] occurs on a very high note, substitute *ah*. When the note is sufficiently high, the substitution will be imperceptible to the listener. The word will sound natural, and the voice will sound free. The singing of a genuine [ɛ] on an extremely high note will result in a pinched tone. The substitution, however, is an expedient to be used only on the highest tones in the singer's voice. It is not licensed for use elsewhere.

Practice singing:

wed	tell	head	guest	any
let	well	bread	friend	many
met	whether	weather	quest	berry
fed	send	tread	said	bury
bed	gentle	instead	says	leopard

Examples in vocal texts:

Death is now a welcome guest. (*Dido and Aeneas;* Tate, Purcell)
It sometimes comes into my head,
That we may dream when we are dead . . .

Then my rest
Would be among the blest
I should forever dream of you.

(*O, That It Were So;* Landor, Bridge)

After the singer is dead
And the maker buried.
Low as the singer lies
In the field of heather,
Songs of his fashion bring
The swains together.
And when the west is red
With the sunset embers,
The lover lingers and sings,
And the maid remembers.

(*Bright Is the Ring of Words;* Stevenson, Vaughan Williams)

32. [ɪ] AS IN IT

The phonetic symbol [ɪ] represents the vowel sound in the word *it*. Examples of other spellings of this sound: *myth, guilt,* the first syllable of *women,* both syllables of *pretty* and *busy.*

Many singers do not differentiate [ɛ], as in *wed,* and [ɪ].
Practice the following, differentiating the [ɛ] words and the [ɪ] words:

[ɛ]	[ɪ]	[ɛ]	[ɪ]
hem	— him	bet	— bit
ten	— tin	let	— lit
tent	— tint	left	— lift
tender	— tinder	mess	— miss
den	— din	petty	— pity
meant	— mint	slept	— slipped
send	— sinned	crept	— crypt
sense	— since	weather	— wither
went	— winter	whether	— whither

SPECIAL NOTE ON *Pen* AND *Pin*

Sometimes it is the influence of a regional pronunciation that causes people to confuse [ɛ] and [ɪ], especially before *m* and *n. Pen* and *pin* are chief victims of this mix-up. *Pen,* an instrument for writing, should be [pɛn]; and *pin,* an instrument for fastening, should be [pɪn].

WHERE HAVE YOU *Been?*

The word *been* is pronounced like *bin* in America, and like *bean* in England. Both are correct in their respective localities. This word should not be pronounced as *ben,* anywhere.

FINAL UNSTRESSED -*y* (OR -*ies*)

Final -*y,* when unstressed, is [ɪ]. The plural form (-*ies*) retains the [ɪ] sound. Verbs ending in unstressed -*y,* such as *carry,* also retain the [ɪ] sound when their endings become -*ies.*
For example:

lily	[ɪ]	lilies	[ɪz]
carry	[ɪ]	carries	[ɪz]

129

Final -y is often rhymed with final *ee* as in *thee*. For example, *memory* and *thee* are coupled; *victory* and *sea, melody* and *me*, etc. However, the pronunciation of the words should not be changed as an accommodation to this convention of versification. Even under these circumstances, unstressed *y* remains [ɪ].

(*y* is sometimes pronounced [ɑɪ], as in *sky, glorify*, etc. See diphthongs, page 167.)

> *Divine . . . Beautiful . . . Pretty . . . Busy . . . Wind*

Divine. The first vowel is frequently mispronounced. It should be [ɪ], not *ee*.

Beautiful. The second syllable should have the [ɪ] sound.

Pretty and busy. Both syllables of each word have the [ɪ] sound: [prɪtɪ] and [bɪzɪ].

Wind (the noun). Except in one instance mentioned on page 192, this word has the [ɪ] sound.

Practice singing:

it	ring	lily	busy	myth
his	sing	lilies	guilt	rhythm
give	bring	lady	build	mystery
gift	fling	ladies	drink	sympathy
limpid	spirit	misery	think	symphony
silk	mirror	victory	brink	women

Ev'ry valley shall be exalted and ev'ry mountain and hill made low. Behold, I tell you a mystery . . .   (*Messiah;* Handel)

O let the sp*i*rit of th*i*s child return, that he again may l*i*ve!
                    (*Elijah;* Mendelssohn)

Oh, some that's good and godly ones, they hold that *i*t's a s*i*n
To troll the jolly bowl around, and let the dollars sp*i*n.
But I'm for toleration, and for dr*i*nking at an *i*nn . . .
                    (*Captain Stratton's Fancy;* Masefield, Deems Taylor)

33. [i] AS IN ME

The phonetic symbol [i] represents the vowel sound in the word *me*. Examples of other spellings: *see, dream, grieve, seize, key, quay,* the first syllable of *people,* and the second syllable of *ravine.* Some singers ask why [i] is the symbol for this vowel. The reason is that the International Phonetic Alphabet, from which the symbols were drawn, originated on the Continent, where this sound is spelled *i.* Practice singing:

me	see	dream	grieve	seize
he	weep	breathe	believe	receive
she	greet	gleam	yield	key
we	queen	plead	shield	people
evening	freedom	reveal	achieve	ravine

Examples in vocal texts:

He shall *speak peace* unto the *heathen.*   (*Messiah;* Handel)

Down by the Sally gardens
My love and I did *meet,*
She passed the Sally gardens
With little snow-white *feet.*
She bid *me* take love *easy,*
As the *leaves* grow on the *tree,*
But I being young and foolish
With her did not *agree*

(*Down by the Sally Gardens;* Yeats, trad.)

DIFFERENTIATION OF [ɛ], [ɪ], [i]

Many singers do not differentiate [ɛ] as in *wed,* [ɪ] as in *it,* and [i] as in *me.* Practice the following words, going across from left to right, and making a clear distinction between the vowel sounds:

[ɛ]	[ɪ]	[i]
bed	bid	bead
dead	did	deed
head	hid	heed
felled	filled	field
lest	list	least

131

[ɛ] (cont.)	[ɪ] (cont.)	[i] (cont.)
met	mitt	meet
sell	sill	seal
set	sit	seat
well	will	weal

ESPECIALLY IMPORTANT: DIFFERENTIATION OF [ɪ] AND [i]

The differentiation of [ɪ] and [i] is an especially critical one, and failure to make it is rather a prevalent fault. To stress the importance of this differentiation, we offer parallel word lists. If the correct distinction is neglected, the results can be startling.

Singers who do not know an [ɪ] from an [i] transform *let me live* into *let me leave,* thus reducing to a common level two sentiments that are identical only in disagreeable domestic dramas. When they sing a love for *hills,* they produce a passion for *heels,* and when they voice laudable sentiments about something that *fills* the heart, they inform their audiences inadvertently about something that *feels* the heart, which is a bit of cardiac manipulation not common to song texts.

Practice the following words:

[ɪ]	[i]	[ɪ]	[i]
live	leave	dip	deep
hills	heels	grin	green
fills	feels	rip	reap
lips	leaps	sick	seek
ship	sheep	sin	seen
still	steal	slip	sleep
win	wean	wick	weak

The italicized words below must have [ɪ], not [i]:
Her *lips* are like fire.
I attempt from love's *sickness* to fly.   (Howard, Purcell)
I saw a *ship* a-sailing . . . (*An Old Song Resung;* Masefield, Dobson)
In the *still* of the night.   (Cole Porter)

The italicized words below must have [i], not [ɪ]:
The *green* of the sea.
Have you *seen* within your soul . . .
The farmer *reaps* the meadow.
We shall *seek* him.
O *sleep* why dost thou *leave* me?   (*O Sleep;* Handel)
Rocked in the cradle of the *deep.*   (Willard, Knight)

34. [æ] AS IN CAT

The phonetic symbol [æ] represents the vowel sound of the word *cat*. This sound is always spelled with the letter *a*.

[æ] is the most frequent sound of stressed *a* in the English language. Many singers have the mistaken idea that it cannot be well sung, and they substitute *ah*, singing *hahnd* for *hand, shahdow* for *shadow, mahn* for *man,* etc. This substitution is incorrect and unacceptable. There is a small special category of words, such as *ask, laugh, dance,* etc., which may properly have what is sometimes called the "broad *ah*," but they are greatly outnumbered by the words that must have [æ]. The "ask words" will be listed in Chapter 48, but at this point we shall discuss only [æ].

A well-produced [æ] can be a beautiful sound. Because it does not exist in German or Italian, it sometimes is overlooked by singers whose training has been devoted chiefly to European vocal literature. But everyone who sings English must master this vowel sound, and it is not difficult to acquire.

Sing the words *head* [ɛ] and *had* [æ] with long, sustained tones. (Remember to sing *head* in a relaxed way, with the lower lip dropped comfortably.) Be careful to differentiate the vowels, but keep the soft palate equally high for both. When the soft palate is lowered, [æ] has a distressing nasal twang.

Some singers find it more helpful to approach [æ] from *ah*. Try this experiment: sing *heart* (without *r*, of course) and *had* with long, sustained tones, again keeping the soft palate equally high for both words. Determine which procedure is more helpful for you in singing a good [æ]: *head — had* or *heart — had*.

Your ear is your best guide in making the distinction between [ɛ] and [æ] and *ah*. There is a slight adjustment of the speech organs for the sound: the sides of the tongue and the corners of the mouth may perhaps widen a bit for [æ]. But these changes are too delicate to be relied on as the decisive factor. The production of [æ] should be governed by the ear, rather than by mechanical means.

After having repeated *head* and *had* (or *heart* and *had*) several

133

times, practice singing:

head — had — heart* — had — head

Make a distinction between the three words, and always keep the soft palate as high for *had* as for the other words.

Now practice singing slowly:

heaven — hallow —hollow — hallow — heaven
set — sat — sot — sat — set
said — sad — sod — sad — said
bend — band — bond — band — bend
petal — patter — potter — patter — petal
meadow — madden — model — madden — meadow
met — mat — mart* — mat — met
men — man — mark* — man — men

[æ] can easily be produced on all but the highest notes of the singer's voice. In the uppermost regions of the scale, the substitution of *ah* is unavoidable. Composers who have a comprehensive understanding of the voice and the characteristics of vowels write their music to make this substitution unnecessary; but occasionally a composer's miscalculation compels the singer to modify the vowel so that he may emit an acceptable high note.

Practice singing:

cat	magic	hand	fashion
hat	hallowed	land	passion
sat	valley	sand	compassion
glad	lamb	stand	that (demonstrative)
sad	lamp	understand	matter
sadness	can	happy	have
shadow	man	capture	ravished
madness	vanish	rapture	dazzle

Examples in vocal texts:

In a field by the river
My love and I did *stand,*
And on my leaning shoulder
She placed her snow-white *hand.*

(*Down by the Sally Gardens;* Yeats, trad.)

Your hair in flowing strands of *black:*
How oft I bid you go, how oft I bid you *back!*

(*The Silence of the Night;* transl. Harris, Jr. and Taylor,
Rachmaninoff)

---

*Remember to omit the *r*.

It *cannot* be joy and *rapture* deep . . .
  (*I Cannot Tell What This Love May Be*, from *Patience;*
                                          Gilbert and Sullivan)

A wand'ring minstrel I —
A thing of shreds and *patches,*
Of *ballads*, songs and *snatches,*
And dreamy lullaby.

                (From *The Mikado;* Gilbert and Sullivan)

SPECIAL NOTE ON *Marry* AND *Merry*

Under the influence of a regional pronunciation, some singers
substitute [ɛ] for [æ] in words like *marry* and *tarry*. They make no
distinction between *marry* and *merry*, *tarry* and *terry*, etc. To them,
Harold is *Herold,* and *Paris* is *Perris.*

If you find that you are likely to transfer this speech characteristic into your singing, practice the list below. It offers examples of
words and names that should have [æ], not [ɛ], in the syllable preceding the *r*.

app*a*rel	b*a*rrow	g*a*rret	n*a*rrow
app*a*rent	c*a*rol	h*a*rrow	p*a*radise
*a*rrant	c*a*rriage	h*a*rry	p*a*rish
*a*rrow	c*a*rrot	l*a*riat	p*a*rrot
b*a*rracks	c*a*rry	m*a*rriage	p*a*rry
b*a*rrel	ch*a*rity	m*a*rry	sp*a*rrow
b*a*rren	emb*a*rrass	n*a*rrate	t*a*rry

Names of People or Places

*A*rab	H*a*rold
B*a*rry	H*a*rriet
C*a*rolina	H*a*rry
C*a*rrie	L*a*rry
C*a*rol	P*a*ris

Examples in vocal texts:
When a merry maiden *marries,*
Sorrow goes and pleasure *tarries.*

                (From *The Gondoliers;* Gilbert and Sullivan)
Still they are *carolled* and said —
On wings they are *carried* . . .

  (*Bright Is the Ring of Words;* Stevenson, Vaughan Williams)

35. [u] AS IN TOO

The phonetic symbol [u] represents the vowel sound in the word *too*. Examples of other spellings of this sound: *do, rude, blew, blue, you, beauty*.

For the first time, we encounter a vowel sound that requires a specific shape of lips. There are only five such vowel sounds:

1. [u] as in *too*
2. [ʊ] as in *full*
3. [o] as in *obey* (unstressed syllable)
4. [ɔ] as in *warm*
5. [ɜ] as in *learn*

The second, third, and fourth of these are also used as part of diphthongs.

SHAPE OF THE LIPS FOR [u]

The lips are protruded into a pout, and rounded, with the rounding extremely small. The lips are almost, but not actually, closed. Keep the sides of the lips narrow, so that their formation is truly circular, not slit-shaped.

Do not sing this vowel with the upper lip pulled downward; the result would give the effect of [u] mixed with *ee*. The upper lip should be protruded well away from the teeth.

SING BASIC *ah*

With protruded, small, rounded lips, narrow at the sides, sing with the normal production for the basic *ah*. Practice singing without interruption: *ah-oo-ah-oo-ah-oo*, making the change from *ah* to *oo* entirely by means of the lips. This effect of the lips' shape in front of *ah* is comparable to the effect brought about by placing square and round frames in front of a spotlight, causing the same stream of light to appear in different forms.

Many singers who try to sing [u] with no regard for the shape of the lips, have difficulty with this vowel. They try to form the [u] in the throat, and it becomes either [ʌ] as in *up*, or [ʊ] as in *full*, or a grunted, squeezed, guttural sound. Try this experiment: sing [u] without protruded, small, rounded, narrow lips and notice the un-

136

musical sounds that result. But when well-produced, [u] is a beautiful vowel.

There are singers who will demur at the above instruction, complaining that they will lose volume if they sing [u] in the proper way. This alleged loss is wholly imaginary. An [u] that is sung with protruded, small, rounded lips is so well projected that it reaches the audience impressively.

Practice singing:

too	cool	do	blew	blue
moon	choose	two	flew	flute
noon	foolish	who	few	huge
soon	gloom	whom	beauty	music
doom	loose	lose	you	mute
pool	soothe	tomb	through	rebuke

Practice the words below, remembering the additional instructions about r before [u] (pages 96-97) which we shall repeat here:

1. Pronounce two flips of the tongue for r before [u].

ruby	roof
rude	room
rule	root
ruler	ruin (this word has two syllables: *ru-in*)

2. Pronounce one flip of the tongue between a consonant and [u].

brute	croon
crucify	groom
crude	prove
frugal	brew
fruit	grew
prudent	cruel (this word has two syllables: *cru-el*)

3. Use the American r in [tru] and [dru].

true	truant	drew
truly	truce	droop
truth	troop	druid (this word has two syllables: *dru-id*)

Examples of [u] in vocal texts:

Thy reb*u*ke hath broken his heart . . . How bea*u*tiful are the
feet of them that preach . . .   (*Messiah;* Handel)
But I being young and f*oo*lish . . .
                        (*Down by the Sally Gardens;* Yeats, trad.)

. . . where is no throng
Of birds at noon-day; and no soft throats
Yield their music to the moon.

(*The Green River;* Douglas, Carpenter)

I shan't be gone long,
You come too.

(*The Pasture;* Frost, Naginski)

36. DANIEL SITTETH

Certain words that have a syllable spelled with *u* or *ew* are subject to two different pronunciations, depending on the pronouncer. For example, *duty* is pronounced *dooty* by some, *dyuty* by others; *dew* is pronounced *doo* by some, *dyew* by others. In such words, the second pronunciation is preferred.

Although many literate and experienced speakers use the *oo* pronunciation, people trained specifically for such branches of public appearance as stage, screen, and radio adopt the *yu* form in their work — including popular music.

The words in question are those in which a syllable spelled with either *u* or *ew* follows any one of these consonants: *d, n, l, s, t,* or *th.* Here is a simple device for remembering these consonants: they are the consonants in the two words *DANIEL SITTETH.* We are not concerned with the identity of Daniel or the fact that he sits in the formal present tense. The simple declarative sentence, DANIEL SITTETH, is merely a useful memory aid.

Let us re-state the principle with some important examples of its application.

SYLLABLES SPELLED WITH *u* OR *ew* ARE PRONOUNCED *yu* AFTER THE CONSONANTS THAT APPEAR IN *DANIEL SITTETH.*

d duty, dew, due, endure, during, duke, induce, dune, etc.

n new, knew, nuisance, numerous, enumerate, etc.

l lute, alluring, illusion, elude, prelude, interlude, salutation, etc.

s suitor, suit, pursuit, sue (verb), ensue, assume, consume, presume, resume, etc.

t tune, Tuesday, tumult, student, stupor, stupid, gratitude, multitude, restitution, etc.

th enthuse, enthusiasm

IMPORTANT EXCEPTION!

When a consonant <u>other than</u> *l* precedes *l* within the same syllable, there is no *y* sound. Note that this does not refer to double *l* (the Daniel Sitteth list above includes words with double *l*). This

139

exception applies only to syllables in which some <u>other</u> consonant precedes *l*.

Examples, all of which have no *y* sound:

Words	Pronunciation
blue, blew, etc.	(*bloo*, etc.)
clue, include, exclude, etc.	(*cloo, inclood, exclood*, etc.)
flute, flew, flue, etc.	(*floot, floo*, etc.)
glue, etc.	(*gloo*, etc.)
plume, plutocrat, etc.	(*ploom, plootocrat*, etc.)
slew, etc.	(*sloo*, etc.)

*   *

*

You may ask why the Daniel Sitteth list excludes *music, cure, few,* etc. It is because there is only one way to pronounce such words. No one says "moosic" for *music,* "coor" for *cure,* "coot" for *cute,* "poor" for *pure,* "aboose" for *abuse,* or "foo" for *few.* The Daniel Sitteth list includes only words that are pronounced in two ways, and indicates the preferred style.

PROLONG THE *y* SOUND

There is one difference between speaking and singing, in the treatment of Daniel Sitteth words: in speaking, the *y* sound is extremely short, but in singing, it must be elongated to *ee,* or it will not be heard at all. Sing *ee-u* almost as if it were two syllables, with the stress on the second vowel. To your audience, as someone has remarked, it will "sound like the sound you want it to sound like."

CONSISTENCY IN SPELLING

Note that all of the Daniel Sitteth words are spelled with either *u* or *ew*. This is one of the rare instances in our study of English diction in which the spelling can be the complete guide. Words spelled with *o* or *oo* are pronounced *oo* without the *ee* sound.

Examples: do, doom, etc.

noon, noose, etc.

loot, loose, lose, etc.

soon, soothe, etc.

to, too, two, tooth, etc.

No *uh* SOUND IN DANIEL SITTETH WORDS

The Daniel Sitteth list does not include words pronounced with *uh,* as in up [ʌ]. Such words do not take the *y* sound.

Examples: dumb, dunce, etc.
                   numb, number, nuptials, etc.
                   lung, lunge, lumber, etc.
                   sun, sung, sum, sumptuous, etc.
                   tub, tuft, tumble, etc.
                   thunder, thumb, thump, etc.

NOTE ABOUT SUSAN

Proper names are sung as they are commonly pronounced, because here a "refinement" would sound academic. In the case of Susan (or Sue or Susanna), this is well exemplified. Most songs about this lady are colloquial, and for these songs, no *y* sound is included. She is plain *Soosan*.

Examples of Daniel Sitteth words in vocal texts:
And suddenly there was with the angel a multit*u*de of the
              heavenly host . . .   (*Messiah;* Handel)
Oh that I kn*ew* where I might find him . . . (*Elijah,* Mendelssohn)

Thy graces that refrain
To do me d*ue* delight . . .   (*Come Again;* Dowland)
Thou art not so unkind
As man's ingratit*u*de . . .
       (*Blow, Blow, Thou Winter Wind;* Shakespeare, Quilter)
Silence will fall like d*ew*s . . .
                          (*Velvet Shoes;* Wylie, Thompson)
I wore clean collars and a brand n*ew su*it
For the pass examination at the Institute.
       (*When I Was a Lad,* from *H.M.S. Pinafore;* Gilbert and Sullivan)

The silv'ry flute (*oo*),
The melancholy l*u*te (*yu*),
Were night owl's hoot (*oo*)
To my low-whispered coo (*oo*) . . .
       (*Were I Thy Bride,* from *The Yeomen of the Guard;* Gilbert and Sullivan)

37. [ʊ] AS IN FULL

The phonetic symbol [ʊ] represents the vowel sound in the word *full*. Examples of other spellings of this sound: *good, could, wolf,* and the first syllable of *woman*.

SHAPE OF THE LIPS

The lips should be moderately protruded, rounded, but with the rounding slightly larger than for [u]. The size of the rounding may be described as medium.

The extent of the rounding is tremendously important in the correct pronunciation of this vowel. If the rounding is as small as it is for [u], the result will be [u], and the sense of many a word will be changed: *full* will become *fool, pull* will become *pool, wood* will be *wooed,* etc.

Practice singing:

full	wood	look	could
pull	good	book	should
put	stood	took	would
bush	hood	brook	wolf
push	foot	crooked	wolves
fulfill	wool	forsook	woman

Examples in vocal texts:

The cr*oo*ked straight . . .

I bring you g*oo*d tidings . . .

He is f*u*ll of heaviness . . .

He l*oo*ked for some to have pity on him.   (*Messiah;* Handel)

On thy b*o*som let me rest.

More I w*ou*ld, but death invades me.

(Dido and Aeneas; Tate, Purcell)

I shall go shod in silk

And you in w*oo*l . . .

(Velvet Shoes; Wylie, Thompson)

And I watch the w*oo*ds grow darker . . .

(By a Lonely Forest Pathway; transl. Chapman, Griffes)

142

38. [o] AS IN OBEY

The phonetic symbol [o] represents the vowel sound in the <u>un-stressed</u> syllable of the word *obey*. The sound appears only in un-stressed syllables, and its identification is simplified by the fact that it is always spelled with the single letter *o*.

When *o* appears in a stressed syllable, it is followed by [ʊ] be-cause it is diphthongized [oʊ]. (See page 171.)

SHAPE OF THE LIPS

The lips should be rounded, with the rounding comparatively large. The protrusion should be very slight.

Contrast the three sounds having rounded lips:

[u] (small)
[ʊ] (medium)
[o] (large)

Practice singing, without interruption:

[u] — [ʊ] — [o] — [ʊ] — [u]

CAUTION

There should be no tightening of the lips for [u], [ʊ], or [o]. There sometimes is a particular tendency to tense the lips in singing [o]. This tension will bring about a "tight" tone.

Practice singing:

		Words having [o] in the second syllable:
obey	provide	memory
omit	protect	immolate
police	profound	desolate
polite	pronounce	omnipotent

143

39. [ɔ] AS IN WARM

The phonetic symbol [ɔ] represents the vowel sound in the word *warm*. Examples of other spellings of this sound: *morn, all, cause, law, daughter, ought, water, broad, broth.*

Remember to omit the *r* in sounding the word *warm*. *Warm* is used as a key word because its vowel has a uniform pronunciation, whereas the vowel in other [ɔ] words is subject to regional variation.

SHAPE OF THE LIPS

The lips should be protruded far forward, in an "oval" shape. The lips should be quite far apart, and narrowed at the corners. Quotation marks have been put around "oval" because the mouth will not <u>look</u> absolutely oval; but you will have the <u>feeling</u> of lips formed in that shape.

This sound is much darker than *ah.*

Practice singing, without interruption, *ah*-[ɔ]-*ah*-[ɔ]-*ah*-[ɔ], making the change from *ah* to [ɔ] entirely by means of the lips. In sounding *ah,* the lips have no prescribed shape, but you will observe that they are not protruded and they are not narrowed into an oval. Practice singing:

warm	all	cause	law	daughter
warn	call	because	awe	taught
warp	small	pause	awful	caught
war	walk	autumn	dawn	aught
swarm	talk	daunt	draw	
	altar	gaunt	claw	ought
morn	exalt	haunt	hawk	fought
lord	always	taunt	saw	bought
storm	also	applaud	jaw	brought
horse	although	Paul	raw	sought
sword	bald	exhaust	flaw	thought

In certain sections of the country, most of these words are pronounced with the sound of *ah* instead of [ɔ]. This localized pronunciation should be changed to the standard pronunciation for public performance.

144

The words in which the regional substitution of *ah* for [ɔ] is likely to occur are those in which the following patterns of spelling are found. Singers who tend to that special mispronunciation will find it important to memorize this list of spellings:

al (also *ald, alk, all, alt*)
au
aw
aught
ought

Note also these words:

water
broad (and its derivatives, such as *abroad, broaden,* etc.)
broth, froth, wroth

For reference, a long list of words that are likely to suffer from this mispronunciation of [ɔ] is furnished in Appendix I.

Examples in vocal texts:

Ev'ry valley shall be ex*a*lted . . .   (*Messiah;* Handel)

He t*a*lketh . . . C*a*ll him louder . . . Dr*aw* near, *a*ll ye people, come to me! . . . Night f*a*lleth round me . . . and the glory of the Lord ever shall rew*a*rd you.   (*Elijah;* Mendelssohn)

A branch of May I br*ou*ght you here . . .

So it's God bless you *a*ll, both great and sm*a*ll . . .
                    (*May Day Carol;* trad. arr. Deems Taylor)

Unlearned he in *au*ght
Save that which love has t*au*ght . . .
I am the l*o*wliest tar
That sails the w*a*ter,
And you, proud maiden, are
The captain's d*au*ghter. (From *H.M.S. Pinafore;* Gilbert and
                                        Sullivan)

40. [ɜ] AS IN LEARN

The phonetic symbol [ɜ] represents the vowel sound in the word *learn*. Examples of other spellings of this sound: *bird, her, word, journey, burn, myrtle*.

The spellings of this sound are varied, but in all of them an *r* is written after the vowel. This *r*, we need hardly remind you, is never pronounced before a consonant. *Learn*, for example, is pronounced [lɜn]; *bird* is [bɜd]. When a word in the [ɜ] category ends in *r*, the word that follows determines whether or not the *r* is to be pronounced. *Her*, in the phrase *her voice*, is [hɜ] without the *r;* in the phrase *her anxiety*, it is [hɜr] with the *r*. (See Basic Rules of *r:* page 9.)

SHAPE OF THE LIPS

Curl the lips outward in the shape of the bell of a French horn or, if you fancy a romantic comparison, of a morning-glory. This lip position should be retained all the way up the scale, opening wider as the voice goes higher, without losing the outward turning of the lips. This is especially important on high notes, because it prevents the vowel from sounding like [ɔ]. For example, the word *yearn* would otherwise sound like *yawn. I am yearning for you* would sound like "I am yawning for you."

Contrast the following:

[ɜ]		[ɔ]	[ɜ]		[ɔ]
learn	—	lawn	worship	—	warship
yearn	—	yawn	word	—	ward
bird	—	board	err	—	oar
firm	—	form	burn	—	born
stir	—	store	turn	—	torn

Be sure not to insert another vowel sound after the [ɜ]. This is a common fault in areas where some people sing *word* [wɜd] as "woid" [wɜɪd].

Practice singing:

learn	her	bird	word	burn
yearn	sermon	girl	world	burden

146

search	serve	whirl	worm	turn
earth	person	twirl	worth	return
dearth	determine	sir	worthy	curl
heard	herd	stir		churn
	mercy	birth		spurn
journey	term	fir	myrtle	fur
sojourn	err	firm	myrrh	unfurl

Examples in vocal texts:

Let the *ea*rth bring forth grass . . . The h*er*b yielding seed . . .
With v*er*dure clad, the fields appear . . .

(*The Creation;* Haydn)

For thou art plenteous in m*er*cy . . . and I am Thy s*er*vant . . .
I have done these things according to Thy w*or*d . . . and let
their hearts again be t*ur*ned.   (*Elijah;* Mendelssohn)

*Jour*neys end in lovers meeting . . .
Present m*ir*th hath present laughter . . .

(*O Mistress Mine;* Shakespeare, Quilter)

The listening w*or*ld in w*or*ship lovelier grows.

(*To One Who Passed Whistling Through the Night;* Agrell,
Gibbs)

When I was a lad I s*er*ved a t*er*m
As office boy to an Att*or*ney's f*ir*m.

(*H.M.S. Pinafore;* Gilbert and Sullivan)

41. [ʌ] AS IN UP

The phonetic symbol [ʌ] represents the vowel sound in the word *up*. Examples of other spellings of this sound: *love, flood, does, trouble.*

There is no specific shape of the lips for this vowel, which is easily produced and rarely presents any problem for the singer. The only possible difficulty is an occasional confusion of [ʌ] with *ah*. Some singers fail to differentiate, for example, between *wonder* and *wander*. Sing these two words and observe that, while neither [ʌ] nor *ah* has any designated shape of the lips, the jaws are wider apart for *ah* than for [ʌ]. It is important to note that the jaws are completely relaxed for both vowels, the only difference being in the distance between them. The entire action is natural. There should be no tenseness in the jaws for [ʌ]. There should be no attempt to wrench them violently apart for *ah*.

Differentiate the following:

[ʌ]	*ah*
come	calm
dull	doll
wonder	wander
Come unto me . . .	The sea is *calm* tonight.
(*Messiah*)	(*Dover Beach;* Arnold, Barber)

I *wonder* as I *wander* out under the sky . . .   (Niles)

Additional words for practice:

up	love	flood	trouble
sun	lover	blood	double
hum	cover	does	young
cup	hover	won	touch
much	mother	one	rough
flung	brother	some	enough

Examples in vocal texts:

And the tongue of the dumb shall sing . . . (*Messiah;* Handel)

148

So this winged hour is dropt to *us* from ab*o*ve . . .
When twofold silence is the song of l*o*ve.
                    (*Silent Noon;* Rossetti, Vaughan Williams)

THE PREFIX *un-*

It is essential that the prefix *un-* have a clearly heard [ʌ] sound, because this prefix is, in itself, at least as important as the rest of the word. *Un-* is a syllable that denies or reverses the meaning of the rest of the word in which it appears. Unless it is definitely audible, the sense of the text is changed completely. And *un-* may often be the source of the dramatic value in a word.
In practicing the following, remember to sound a double *n:*

unkind	unknown	untold
unhappy	unwilling	unrewarded
unfortunate	untroubled	unsung

. . . the ears of the deaf *un*stopped . . .   (*Messiah;* Handel)

hurry AND *worry*, ETC.

When the following words appear in works that require a British accent, their stressed syllable should have the sound of [ʌ]:

hurry	*cour*age
worry	en*cour*age
scurry	*flour*ish
flurry *furrow*	*nour*ish

42. [ə]: THE NEUTRAL VOWEL

The phonetic symbol [ə] represents the vowel sound of the second syllable of *sofa*. This sound may be indicated in spelling by many vowels or combinations of vowels. Here are a few examples of various spellings: the first syllable of *enchant;* the second syllable of *sailor, gladness, nation, ocean, patience, joyous, circus;* the third syllable of *loneliness, covenant,* etc.

This vowel sound is called the neutral vowel. It is also known as the indefinite vowel, the obscured vowel, and the vowel murmur.

In general, the neutral vowel is pronounced in singing as it is in speech.

THE NEUTRAL VOWEL IS ALWAYS UNSTRESSED

The neutral vowel appears only in an unstressed syllable — never in a stressed syllable. As illustration, consider the word *entrance.* When the first syllable is accented (EN-*trance,* meaning *entry*), the second syllable is unaccented and has the neutral vowel; when the second syllable is accented (*en*-TRANCE, meaning *enrapture*), the first syllable is unaccented and has the neutral vowel.

The neutral vowel cannot be practiced as an isolated sound, detached from a word or phrase. It can only be pronounced properly in its context. Any attempt to sound it as a separate entity would stress it; and its chief characteristic is lack of stress.

It is extremely important to examine carefully the following lists of words that demonstrate the neutral vowel. This is the simplest and most effective method of becoming familiar with this sound in its varied and limitless spellings. In the illustrations below, the neutral vowel has been italicized.

sadn*e*ss	rapt*u*re	dear*e*st	ang*e*l	comf*o*rt	pass*io*n
need*e*d	pet*a*l	mom*e*nt	heav*e*n	end*e*th	pleas*a*nt
nev*e*r	crims*o*n	aut*u*mn	homew*a*rd	phant*o*m	treas*u*re
trait*o*r	hopel*e*ss	sol*e*mn	pres*e*nce	purp*o*se	kingd*o*m
nect*a*r	sheph*e*rd	qui*e*t	hands*o*me	tit*a*n	en*e*my
murm*u*r	men*a*ce	ri*o*t	Christm*a*s	for*ei*gn	proph*e*sy
ros*e*s	woodl*a*nd	id*o*l	pat*ie*nce	oc*ea*n	dial*e*ct

150

Words like *sudden, people,* and *little,* which, when spoken, are pronounced *sudd'n, peop'l,* and *litt'l,* are sung with a neutral vowel between the last two consonants.

sudden [dən]	people [pəl]	little [təl]
maiden [dən]	table [bəl]	*idle [dəl]

In singing contractions, as in *wouldn't,* sing a neutral vowel between the *d* and *n.*

wouldn't	(wouldent)
hadn't	(hadent)
didn't	(dident)

Exception: In lyrics of popular, or dialect, or extremely colloquial songs, the neutral vowel between contracted *d* and *n* is omitted for reasons of style.

Examples of two neutral vowels in one word:

shepherdess	firmament	governor	
helplessness	covenant	lovable	(lovabel)
cleverest	excellent	**diamond	(di-a-mond)

(Need we remark that none of our illustrative lists is complete? A full catalogue of words having the neutral vowel would make this manual burdensome to carry, but enough specimens are offered to suggest the many forms in which the neutral vowel appears.)

A NEUTRAL VOWEL SYLLABLE CAN BE SUSTAINED

Even though a neutral vowel syllable is always unstressed, it can be prolonged when the musical setting demands that it be sustained. Turn back to the lists of words and practice singing some of them on long notes. Then practice singing them with more than one note to a syllable.

UNSTRESSED MONOSYLLABLES

In addition to the unstressed syllables which we have illustrated, there are many unstressed words of one syllable whose vowel sound is usually the neutral vowel. These include some of the pronouns, auxiliary verbs, prepositions, and other connectives.

If we compare a phrase to a string of beads, the connective words are comparable to the string, and the important words, those that give the meaning, are like the beads. The string that holds the beads together is inconspicuous, and we focus our attention on the

---

Idle and *idol* are pronounced alike.
**Note that *diamond* has three syllables.

beads. In the same way, the connecting words remain unobtrusively in the background while we concentrate our attention on the words that present the ideas. We do not swallow or mumble these words; we merely pronounce them with the neutral vowel. This helps to make the important words stand out more clearly, and to maintain the lyrical and musical curve of the phrase.

The following monosyllables are <u>always</u> sung with a neutral vowel:

the before a consonant
    (Before a vowel sound, *the* is pronounced as *thee* [i].)
a before a consonant
    (Never sing *a* as *ay*.)
an before a vowel sound

The following monosyllables have a neutral vowel unless they are greatly expanded by the music, in which case they are sung with a full vowel (the sound as spelled).

and [ə] on short notes; full vowel [æ] on long notes
as [ə] on short notes; full vowel [æ] on long notes
of [ə] on short notes; full vowel [ʌ] on long notes
than [ə] on short notes; full vowel [æ] on long notes

MONOSYLLABLES HAVING TWO FORMS: WEAK AND STRONG

Many monosyllables have weak (unstressed) and strong (stressed) forms, the choice of which is determined by the meaning of the phrase in which they occur. In the weak form, they have the neutral vowel; in the strong form, they have the full vowel sound. Here are a few examples:

Weak Form with Neutral Vowel [ə]	Strong Form with Full Vowel	
(*for*) We hope for peace.	What are you searching for?	[ɔ]
(*am*) I am hoping . . .	Here I am.	[æ]
(*can*) I can see it plainly.	Go, if you can.	[æ]
(*has*) Everyone has gone.	Who has it?	[æ]
(*have*) He may have lost it.	Indeed, I have!	[æ]
(*them*) He found them wandering.	Not for you, but for them.	[ɛ]
(*some*) We shall hear some music.	Some have arrived.	[ʌ]

There are occasions when you will have to make a temporary departure from the principle of letting the meaning determine the form to be used. If the composer has placed a long, sustained note on a weak form monosyllable, you must reverse the Duchess's moral and "take care of the sounds and the sense will take care of itself." You are virtually forced to use the strong form.

In words of <u>more than one syllable</u>, however, you are not obliged to forsake the neutral vowel, even on a long, sustained note.

THE WORD *that*

Grammatically speaking, the word *that* may be a conjunction, or it may have a relative or demonstrative function. When it is a conjunction or a relative word, it has the neutral vowel [ə]; when it is a demonstrative word, it has the vowel [æ].

Conjunction [ə]
    I think that I shall go.
    Oh, that it were so!

Relative [ə]   Demonstrative [æ]
    The song that I sang . . .   That song is beautiful.
    The evil that men do . . .   That is evil.

Occasionally, a phrase includes two forms of *that:*
Not that that would very much grieve me.
    [ə] [æ]   (*Don't Come In, Sir, Please;* Giles, Scott)
For it's that that makes the bonny drink . . .
    [æ] [ə]   (*Captain Stratton's Fancy;* Masefield, Taylor)

THE PREPOSITION *to*

The preposition *to* is usually unstressed and, in its normal pronunciation, has the neutral vowel [ə] before a consonant, and [ʊ] before a vowel. When it is prolonged by the music, it should have [ʊ], even before a consonant. If it is sustained to the duration of, let us say, a whole measure, it may be advisable to sing the vowel [u], as in *too.*

THE SPECIAL VALUE OF THE NEUTRAL VOWEL

The recognition and proper pronunciation of the neutral vowel is tremendously important to every artist. The principle of non-stress of unaccented syllables by means of the neutral vowel is an integral part of the English language. Without it, there can be no fluent, natural, and effective speaking or singing of English. Furthermore, there can be no understandable diction when there is such distortion. Anyone who ignores neutral vowels, pronouncing rigidly according to spelling, and tries to give equal weight to every word and syllable, sounds as if he were an eager participant in a spelling bee — with approximately the same expressive intelligence and appeal that is apparent when he spells out m-o-n-u-m-e-n-t for the judges. The results of such efforts are pedantic, stilted performances. The curve of the phrase, both literary and musical, is absent. A singer who sings "Now sleeps thah crimsahn petahl, now thah white" instead of "Now sleeps the crimson petal, now the white" appears to be without style and feeling. He sounds like a child reading aloud from a primer. "Angel [εl] of heaven [εn]" can never sound as natural and beautiful as "angel of heaven." "Pleas-ant [ænt] play-sez [sεz]" seems to be something unintelligible about the insect world, instead of "pleasant places." *Menace* is not *men* plus *ace* (as in a deck of cards), but [mεnəs]. There is no *fort* in *comfort,* no *rest* in *dearest;* no one is *dead* in *needed.* There is a word, known in every stratum of musical criticism, that characterizes this sort of performance: "square." To be musically square is as unfortunate as it is laudable to be ethically square.

A helpful prescription against squareness in music might read like this: Syllables must be sung as part of a word. Words must be sung as part of a phrase. Unstressed syllables must be unstressed. And neutral vowels must be neutral.

SUMMARY OF UNSTRESSED SYLLABLES
HAVING NEUTRAL VOWEL [ə]

In polysyllables (even when sustained)
Monosyllables: *the, a, an*
               and, as, of, than (unless greatly prolonged)
               Weak form of many words (unless greatly prolonged)
               that (conjunctive or relative)
               to (in one instance)

Examples in vocal texts (remember that we italicize the neutral vowel or syllable):

Comf*o*rt ye, my peo*p*le, speak ye comfort*a*bly to [tʊ] Jerus*a*lem . . . Th*e* voice of him th*a*t crieth in th*e* wilderness . . . Ev'ry valley shall be *e*xalt*e*d *a*nd ev'ry mount*ai*n *a*nd hill made low . . . the crook*e*d straight *a*nd th*e* rough plac*e*s plain . . . Oh, thou th*a*t tell*e*st good tidings to [tʊ] Zion . . . *A*nd sudd*e*nly there was with the ang*e*l *a* multitude *o*f the heav*e*nly host . . . Come unto Him, all ye th*a*t

labo*ur* . . . Why do th*e* nations so furio*us*ly rage togeth*er* . . . We
sh*a*ll all be changed in *a* mom*e*nt at th*e* last trump*e*t.
(Messiah; Handel)

Fr*o*m th*e* rage *o*f the temp*e*st,
Out *o*f th*e* seething wat*er*s,
So far th*e* gods protect me;
Here, in this lonely hav*e*n,
I kneel *a*nd thank th*e* gods f*o*r their assist*a*nce!
But what avails this thread *o*f mere *e*xistence . . .
Alone in these deathlike reg*io*ns . . .
(Recit. from Julius Caesar; Handel)
Now I teach my childr*e*n each melodi*ou*s meas*u*re.
Oft th*e* tears are flowing . . . from my mem'ry's treas*u*re.
(Songs My Mother Taught Me; MacFarren, Dvořák)
Now sleeps th*e* crimson pet*a*l, now th*e* white;
Nor waves th*e* cypr*e*ss in th*e* pal*a*ce walk;
   Nor winks th*e* gold fin in th*e* porph'ry font:
Th*e* firefly wak*e*ns: waken thou with me.
Now folds th*e* lily all her sweetn*e*ss up,
*A*nd slips int*o* th*e* bosom *o*f th*e* lake;
So fold thyself, my dear*e*st, thou, *a*nd slip
Into [tʊ] my bos*o*m *a*nd be lost in me.
(Now Sleeps the Crimson Petal; Tennyson, Quilter)

43. UNSTRESSED SYLLABLES THAT DO NOT HAVE THE NEUTRAL VOWEL

Although most unstressed syllables have the neutral vowel, there are some that have other sounds.

UNSTRESSED SYLLABLES WHOSE VOWEL SOUND IS SPELLED WITH THE SINGLE LETTER *i*

An unstressed syllable whose vowel sound is spelled with the single* letter *i* is pronounced [ɪ], as in *it*. This is also true of unstressed monosyllables with this spelling.

In the examples given below and in other instances in this chapter, we place the phonetic symbol [ɪ] within the words, and dispense with the usual brackets:

wɪth	ruɪn	doɪng	dɪvine	ɪmagɪne
ɪn	musɪc	walkɪng	ɪmplore	ɪmɪtate
	spirɪt	singɪng	ɪnvite	primɪtɪve

In the following examples, the second syllable has [ɪ], and the last syllable is sung with a neutral vowel (which we italicize as usual):

happɪn*ess*	delɪc*ate*
lonelɪn*ess*	sacrɪl*ege*
lovelɪn*ess*	citɪz*en*

SPECIAL NOTE ON *beautiful*

The second syllable of *beautiful* has [ɪ], and the third syllable has [ʊ], as in *full*. Do not use the neutral vowel in any of the syllables of this word.

SPECIAL NOTE ON *evil*

In speech, there is no vowel sound between the *v* and *l* of the word *evil*. It is *ev'l*. But because the singing voice requires a vowel for every syllable, the second syllable of *evil*, when sung, has the vowel [ɪ].

---

*The second syllable of *passion, patience*, etc., has the neutral vowel. (See page 150.) Note that the vowel sound in such syllables is spelled with *i* plus another vowel.

UNSTRESSED FINAL y (OR -ies)

Remember that unstressed final *y* is [ɪ]. (See p. 27.) When the addition of *s* changes the spelling to *-ies,* the [ɪ] sound is retained. Examples:

lady	ladies
carry	carries

PREFIXES

When the neutral vowel occurs in a prefix, its treatment is governed by the length of the note. If the vowel is as short as it would be in speaking — approximately the equivalent of a 16th note — it is sung as a neutral vowel. If the note is of longer duration, the vowel must be modified.

The following material concerning prefixes applies to prefixes only. Within a polysyllabic word, prefixes are the only unstressed syllables that require any modification when sustained. Other unstressed syllables maintain the neutral vowel whatever their duration.

When sung on notes longer than a 16th:

Prefixes ending in *e* or consisting of *e* alone are sung as [ɪ].

Prefixes spelled with *a* are sung as [ʌ], as in *up.*

On 16th notes or less, all of the above have the neutral vowel.

PREFIXES ENDING IN *e* OR CONSISTING OF *e* ALONE
(SUNG AS [ɪ] WHEN LONGER THAN A 16TH NOTE)

These include:

de-	as in	*delight*
re-	as in	*remember*
pre-	as in	*prepare*
be-	as in	*beloved*
se-	as in	*serene*
e-	as in	*emotion*

THE PREFIX *de-*

The prefix *de-* should never be pronounced as *dee-* unless it signifies a kind of severance from what is expressed by the rest of the word. In this case, the prefix receives a slight accentuation. For example, the pronunciation *dee-* is correct when we *defrost* the refrigerator, *derail* a train, *decode* a message. But we do not remove a light when we are *delighted;* our franchise is not taken from us when we are *devoted;* and *desire* is not ordinarily defined as a removal from one's father.

Sing:			Also, sing:		
dɪlight,	not *dee-light*		despair as	dɪ-spair	
dɪvotion,	not *dee-votion*		despise as	dɪ-spise	
dɪsire,	not *dee-sire*		destroy as	dɪ-stroy	
dɪceive,	not *dee-ceive*		despite as	dɪ-spite	
	etc.			etc.	

THE PREFIX *re-*

The prefix *re-* should never be pronounced *ree-* unless it means a repetition of the action in the remainder of the word, in which case it has a secondary accent. For example, *ree-* is correct when we *re-pack* a trunk, *re-tread* a tire, *re-echo* a sound. But we do not *member* again when we *remember;* we do not *vere* again when we *revere;* and we gather no additional *morse* when we suffer *remorse.*

Sing:	rɪmember,	not *ree-member*
	rɪvere,	not *ree-vere*
	rɪmorse,	not *ree-morse*
	rɪceive,	not *ree-ceive*
	etc.	

THE PREFIX *pre-*

The prefix *pre-* should never be pronounced *pree-* unless it means "in advance," in which case it has a secondary accent. For example, *pree-* is correct when we *prepay* a package, or *preheat* an oven. But we do not *pare* in advance when we *prepare* a speech; we do not *fer* in advance when we *prefer* something; we do not *tend* ahead of time when we *pretend.*

Sing:	prɪpare,	not *pree-pare*
	prɪfer,	not *pree-fer*
	prɪtend,	not *pree-tend*
	etc.	

THE PREFIXES: *be-, se-,* AND *e-*

The prefixes *be-, se-,* and *e-* should not have the *ee* vowel. This would seem artificial and pedantic.

Sing:	bɪloved,	not *bee-loved*		sɪrene,	not *see-rene*
	bɪlieve,	not *bee-lieve*		sɪvere,	not *see-vere*
	bɪside,	not *bee-side*			etc.
	bɪcause,	not *bee-cause*			
	bɪfore,	not *bee-fore*		ɪmotion,	not *ee-motion*
	bɪtween,	not *bee-tween*		ɪvade,	not *ee-vade*
	etc.				etc.

WHEN THE PREFIX CONSISTS OF *e* PLUS A CONSONANT

Prefixes like *em-*, *en-*, *es-*, *ex-*, and others made up of *e* plus a following consonant are sung with the neutral vowel, except when the prefix continues through more than one note, as in some classical airs from oratorios and other sources. In such circumstances, sing [ɛ] instead of the neutral vowel. When these prefixes are sung on only one note, it is easy to shorten the neutral vowel by anticipating the consonant.

PREFIXES SPELLED WITH *a*
(SUNG AS *uh* [ʌ] WHEN LONGER THAN A 16TH NOTE)

These include:

a-   as in *away*
at-   as in *attempt*
ca-   as in *caress*
la-   as in *lament*   and many more.

When these prefixes are longer than a 16th note, they tempt many a singer to use the vowels *ay* or [æ] or *ah*.

These pronunciations sound far more artificial than the vowel [ʌ] which is more closely related to the neutral vowel. For visual simplicity, we shall re-spell them with *uh*.

Sing: *uh*way,   not *ay-way*
       *uh*ttempt,   not [æ]-*tempt*
       c*uh*ress,   not *cah-ress*
       l*uh*ment,   not *lah-ment*

THE PREFIXES *Sur-* AND *Per-*
(PRONOUNCED [ɜ], AS IN *Learn*)

The prefixes *sur-* and *per-* are sung with the vowel [ɜ], as in *learn*. (See Chapter 40.) Of course, the *r* is omitted. Although in speech some of these prefixes have [ɜ] and some have the neutral vowel, in singing they all have [ɜ] because of the musical elongation of the syllable.

Examples:

surprise	perhaps
surpass	perform
survey	perplex

THE PREFIX *Ful-*

The prefix *ful-* has the sound [ʊ], as in *full*.

UNSTRESSED o

Unstressed *o* is pronounced [o], as in *obey*, whether it is a prefix or a later syllable.
Examples:

obey	memory
provide	melody
polite	desolate

Exception: The prefixes *com-* and *con-* have the vowel [ʌ], as in *up*.

command	console
commit	confide

THE UNSTRESSED SUFFIX -ow

The unstressed suffix (final syllable) *-ow*, as in *sorrow*, is not pronounced with the neutral vowel. It has the diphthong [oʊ], as in *no*. (See page 171.)
Examples:

sorrow	meadow	window
sparrow	follow	fellow
arrow	hollow	pillow
borrow	hallow	billow
furrow	swallow	winnow

SECONDARY ACCENTS DO NOT HAVE THE NEUTRAL VOWEL

By way of amplifying previous reference to secondary accents, we note here that a secondary accent is one that receives a weaker stress than the primary accent, but is not completely unaccented.

Syllables receiving secondary accents do not have the neutral vowel, but are pronounced with a full vowel sound.

In the examples given below, we indicate the chief or primary accent with a heavy mark (′) and the secondary accent with a lighter mark (′). The unaccented syllables are italicized.

The sound of a syllable with secondary accent differs from the sound of the identical syllable when it has no accent whatever. Note this in the examples given below:

Syllable	With Secondary Accent	Full Vowel Sound	With No Accent	Neutral Vowel
al-	al'-*ter*-ca'-*tion*	[ɔ]	pet-*al*	[ə]
ar-	ar'-*ti*-fi'-*cial*	[ɑ]	beg-*gar-ly*	[ə]
en-	en'-*ter*-tain'	[ɛ]	heav-*en*	[ə]
un-	un'-hap'-*py*	[ʌ]	vol-*un*-teer	[ə]

We recall to your attention the importance of the prefix *un-* (see page 149). It must have the full vowel sound [ʌ]. *Unhappy* must not sound like *a happy*.

SUMMARY OF UNSTRESSED SYLLABLES
THAT DO NOT HAVE THE NEUTRAL VOWEL

Those having single vowel spelled with

i or *y*	sung as [ɪ]
Prefixes: Ending in *e-* or consisting of *e-* alone	sung as [ɪ]

de-   be-
re-   se-
pre-   e-

Beginning with *e* plus consonant
   (*em-*, *en-*, etc.)

On more than one note	sung as [ɛ]
(otherwise, sung as [ə])	
Spelled with *a*	sung as [ʌ]

a-   ca-
at-   la-
etc.

Unstressed *o*	sung as [o]
Except prefixes *com-* and *con-*	sung as [ʌ]
Unstressed suffix *-ow*	sung as [oʊ]
Secondary accents	sung with full vowel
Note especially prefix *un-*	sung as [ʌ]

In the following examples, the neutral vowel is italicized, the symbol [ɪ] is included in the word, without brackets, the prefix *a-* is respelled with *uh* for visual simplicity:

Prɪpare thyself, Zi*on*, wɪth tender uhffecti*on*,
Th*e* pur*est*, th*e* fair*est*, this day to [tʊ] rɪceive.
(Christmas Oratorio; Bach)

For bɪhold, darkn*ess* shall cover the earth . . . Rɪjoice greatly, O daught*er* of Zion . . . He was dɪspisèd *a*nd rɪjected . . . Thy rɪbuke h*a*th broken his heart; He is full *o*f heavɪn*ess* . . . I know th*a*t my Rɪdeem*er* liveth . . . *a*nd though worms dɪstroy this body . . .
(Messiah; Handel)

Wɪth verdur*e* clad, th*e* fields uhppear dɪlightful to th*e* ravɪshed sense.
(The Creation; Haydn)

Hear ye, Israel; hear what th*e* Lord speak*eth* "Oh hadst thou heed*ed* my commandm*ents*!" Who hath bɪlievèd our rɪport; to whom

is the arm of the Lord rɪvealèd? . . . thou art uhfraid of a man
that shall die; and forgettest the Lord thy Maker, who hath stretchèd
forth the heavens, and laid the earth's foundations . . . It is ɪnough,
O Lord now take uhway my life for I am not better than my
fathers . . . I dɪsire to [tʊ] live no longer . . . for my days are but
vanɪtɪ . . .   (*Elijah;* Mendelssohn)

  She never told her love;
  But let concealment, like a worm ɪ' the bud,
  Feed on her damask cheek.
  She sat, like Patience on a monument,
  Smilɪng at grief.

                    (*She Never Told Her Love;* Shakespeare, Haydn)

44. [a], [ɒ], [e]:
WHY WE DO NOT SING THEM

Three of the symbols in the phonetic alphabet, [a], [ɒ], and [e], have been included for the sake of completeness, but we have found that they may be omitted from the singer's list of vowels.

[a] AS IN *Ask* (AS SOMETIMES SPOKEN)

The phonetic symbol [a] represents a sound called the intermediate *a* because it is between [ɑ] as in *ah* and [æ] as in *cat*.

It is used by some speakers in a group of words often called the "ask words." (This group will be fully discussed in Chapter 48.) But even in the pronunciation of the *ask* words, there is little uniformity. In Southern England where these words regularly have a "broad *ah*," some speakers use [ɑ] and others use [a].

When English is sung, the shadings of [ɑ] and [a] are so nearly alike as to be imperceptible to the audience.

For these two reasons — the lack of uniformity in speech and the virtual identity of [ɑ] and [a] when sung — the singer will find it practical to ignore [a] in the vocalization of English.

In some other languages the exact shading of [a] is more precisely specified, but constant tests have indicated that in singing English, this shading is largely theoretical.

[ɒ] AS IN *Hot* (SOUTH ENGLAND)

The symbol [ɒ] represents the sound of the word *hot* in the speech of Britons (principally from the south of England) and some Americans. It is half-way between [ɔ], as in *warm*, and [ɑ], as in *ah*, and is always quick and crisp.

Because the pace of music is almost invariably slower than that of speech, [ɒ] must be elongated in song, and, in this elongation, it loses its two principal characteristics: its crispness and its true vowel sound, for it is changed either to [ɔ] or to *ah*. We have found that it is best not to attempt this vowel in singing (except in such special instances as Gilbert and Sullivan patter songs).

163

Among words in which [ɒ] occurs are the following, and it is recommended that the *ah* sound be used in singing them:

sorry	song	wash	scoff
forest	long	watch	offer
horror	throng	gospel	office
horrid	gone	god	orange
blossom	want	odd	hot

[e] AS IN *Ate* (WHEN SPOKEN)

The symbol [e] represents the vowel sound in speech of the word *ate* and the vowel sounds in the French word *été*.

This sound is important in spoken English and in the singing of other languages, but we have found that in singing English, [e] is so "closed" that it tends to emerge as *ee* [i]. It is therefore best to replace [e] by the diphthong [ɛɪ]. (See page 168.) This substitution brings to the listener the sound that is actually intended.

45. DIPHTHONGS

Diphthong (pronounced *dif-thong*) is a word derived from the Greek *di-* (meaning *twice*) and *phthongos* (meaning *sound*).

A diphthong is a sound composed of two consecutive vowels in the same syllable. The two vowels are connected without interruption in a continuous sound. The first vowel is sustained, and the second is added at the very end. For example, in the word *night*, the vowel sound is a joining of the vowels [ɑ] as in *ah* and [ɪ] as in *it*. The vowel sound begins with [ɑ] and ends in [ɪ], and the pronunciation of the entire word is indicated phonetically as [nɑɪt]. If the [ɪ] is omitted, the word emerges as *not*.

Diphthongs must be studied carefully and understood thoroughly by singers. Many a vocalist who pronounces diphthongs accurately in speech, apparently as a matter of course, is likely to commit one of two errors when he encounters them in song. The two errors are:

1) Distortion of one of the vowels. One frequently hears singers who befoul the vowel by starting with the wrong sound, which brings about such tonal illiteracies as *toim* for *time, though* for *thou, dee* for *day*. The vocalist who fosters this distortion may not be aware of it until the matter is mentioned to him by a listener. But the distortion would never take place if the singer understood the composition of the diphthong.

2) Omission of the second vowel. Because the pace of singing is slower than that of speech, the singer, rightly, makes a point of sustaining the first vowel; but he neglects to add the second vowel — an oversight of which he would not be guilty in conversation.

In every diphthong, the first vowel is the longer. When the syllable is sung on more than one note, the first vowel is sustained on all the notes, and the second vowel added at the very end of the last note.

To illustrate, the word *night* is sung as follows:

Remember that there should be no break between the two vowels. After the first vowel has been sustained, it blends into the second. In fact, the second vowel is often called a fade or vanish.

There should be no obvious contrast between the two vowels; the change from one into the other should be subtle and almost imperceptible, as it is in speech.

Before studying each diphthong, let us review the particular vowel sounds from which they are formed. We have assembled them in the list given below. Any vowels that do not appear in this list do not appear in diphthongs. It will be a great convenience in studying diphthongs to be completely familiar with the phonetic symbols of the following vowel sounds:

[ɑ] as in *ah*
[ɪ] as in *it*
[ɛ] as in *wed*
[ɔ] as in *warm*
[ʊ] as in *full*
[o] as in the first syllable of *obey* (unstressed)
[ə] as in the second syllable of *sofa* (unstressed; the neutral vowel)

Observe that [i] as in *me* and [u] as in *too* are among the sounds omitted. It will be especially helpful to remember that [i] and [u] do not appear in diphthongs.

46. THE FIRST FIVE DIPHTHONGS

Diphthong		Key Word
[ɑɪ]	as in	*night*
[ɛɪ]	as in	*day*
[ɔɪ]	as in	*boy*
[ɑʊ]	as in	*now*
[oʊ]	as in	*no*

Memorize the key words. They can be remembered easily if they are considered to be the plot of a little story, with a question mark after *now*.

[ɑɪ] AS IN *Night*

The phonetic symbols [ɑɪ] represent the diphthong that is the vowel sound in the word *night*. It is composed of [ɑ], as in *ah*, plus [ɪ], as in *it*. Examples of other spellings of this diphthong: *time, mind, guide, my, eye, bye, buy, aisle, isle, height, lie, sign.*

Avoid these errors:

Do not darken the first vowel to [ɔ], singing *noit, toim,* etc. If you sing the first vowel with protruded, oval lips, you will automatically sing [ɔ], instead of [ɑ].

Do not omit the second vowel, singing *naht, tahm,* etc. This is a regional pronunciation.

Observe that the second vowel is [ɪ], as in *it*, not [i], as in *me*.

Practice singing:

night	time	mind	my	eye	lie
light	thine	kind	thy	rye	die
bright	mine	find	cry	bye	cried
mighty	life	wind (verb)	try	buy	tries
sigh	divine	guide	rhyme	aisle	denies
high	confide	quite	defy	isle	sign
delight	silence	beguile	deny	height	resign

167

Examples in vocal texts:

Drink to me only with th*i*ne *ey*es,
And *I* will pledge with m*i*ne;
Or leave a kiss but in the cup
And *I'll* not look for w*i*ne.
The thirst that from the soul doth r*i*se
Doth ask a drink div*i*ne;
But m*i*ght *I* of Jove's nectar sup,
I would not change for th*i*ne.

(*Drink to Me Only with Thine Eyes;* Ben Jonson)

There is a lady sweet and k*i*nd
Was never face so pleased my m*i*nd
I did but see her passing by
And yet *I* love her till *I* d*i*e.

(*There Is a Lady Sweet and Kind;* Thomas Ford, many settings)

[ɛɪ] AS IN *Day*

The phonetic symbols [ɛɪ] represent the diphthong that is the vowel sound in the word *day*. It is composed of [ɛ], as in *wed*, plus [ɪ], as in *it*. Examples of other spellings of this diphthong: *same, maid, they, veil, great, reign, sleigh.*

First, sing [ɛ] with relaxed, dropped lower lip. At the very end of the syllable, change the [ɛ] to [ɪ]. Observe that the second vowel is [ɪ], as in *it*, not [i], as in *me*.

In speech, the words under discussion are pronounced with [e] or [eɪ], but in the elongated syllables of song, the relaxed [ɛɪ] is preferable. This departure from speech pronunciation actually results in a faithful reproduction in song of the desired sound and makes available to the singer greater beauty of tone. By some acoustical vagary, [e] or [eɪ], when sung in English, sounds so much like [i] that it changes the sense of the word. The master of his *fate* becomes merely the master of his *feet*.

For example, everyone has heard singers who sound the words in the first column below like the words in the second column. Examine the following columns carefully. Then practice them — but only the words in the first column!

Word Intended [ɛɪ]	Wrong Word Often Sung [i]
fate	feet
fade	feed
May	me
wave	weave
pale	peel
say	see
play	plea
hate	heat
veil	veal

The heaven such *grace* did lend her (*Who is Sylvia;* Shakespeare, Schubert)

The heaven such *grease* did lend her.

Waken thou with me. (*Now Sleeps the Crimson Petal;* Tennyson, Quilter)

Weaken thou with me.

All of the words in the lists below have [ɛɪ]. Practice singing:

day	same	maid	they
pray	rage	afraid	obey
gray	face	vain	great
away	late	rain	break
stay	flame	pain	reign
betray	radiant	disdain	feign
dismay	grateful	proclaim	sleigh

Examples in vocal texts:

I attempt from love's sickness to fly in v*a*in,
Since I am myself my own fever and p*a*in . . .
For love has more pow'r and less mercy than f*a*te
To m*a*ke us seek ruin and love those that h*a*te.

(*I Attempt from Love's Sickness to Fly;* Howard, Purcell)

Ah, love, but a d*a*y,
And the world has ch*a*nged.
The sun's aw*a*y, and the bird estr*a*nged;
The wind has dropped and the sky's der*a*nged.

(*Ah, Love! But a Day;* Protheroe, Beach)

Let us walk in the white snow
In a soundless sp*a*ce;
With footsteps quiet and slow,
At a tranquil p*a*ce,
Under v*a*ils of white l*a*ce. (*Velvet Shoes;* Wylie, Thompson)

[ɔɪ] AS IN *Boy*

The phonetic symbols [ɔɪ] represent the diphthong that is the vowel sound in the word *boy*. It is composed of [ɔ], as in *warm*, plus [ɪ] as in *it*. Example of other spelling of this diphthong: *voice*.

Protrude the lips in an oval shape to sound the [ɔ]. Failure to protrude the lips results in the substitution of [ɑ] for [ɔ]. The word *voice* [ɔɪ] becomes *vice* [ɑɪ].

Do not omit the second vowel. Singers who fail to sound the [ɪ] sing *jaw* for *joy* and *gnaws* for *noise*. Observe that the second vowel is [ɪ], not [i].

Practice singing:

boy	annoy	loyal	voice
joy	enjoy	royal	choice
toy	employ	destroy	rejoice

Examples in vocal texts:
The *voice* of him who crieth in the wilderness . . .
    Rejoice, rejoice, rejoice greatly . . .   (*Messiah,* Handel)
O Lord, Thou hast overthrown Thine enemies and *destroyed* them . . . *Joy* on their heads shall be forever lasting.
                             (*Elijah;* Mendelssohn)

[ɑʊ] AS IN *Now*

The phonetic symbols [ɑʊ] represent the diphthong that is the vowel sound in the word *now*. It is composed of [ɑ], as in *ah*, plus [ʊ], as in *full*. Examples of other spellings of this diphthong: *thou, bough.*

Do not begin this diphthong with [o] instead of [ɑ], singing *no* in place of *now*, or *though* in place of *thou*. This is a common inaccuracy which may be due to the fact that all of these words are spelled with *o*. When a singer whose knowledge of English is rudimentary bungles this diphthong, one may sympathize with his struggle with a new language; but no English-speaking singer, who is well aware that these words should be pronounced with [ɑʊ], can be pardoned for substituting [oʊ].

For example:

Word Intended [ɑʊ]	Wrong Word Often Sung [oʊ]
now	no
thou	though
how	hoe
found	phoned

Observe that the second vowel of the diphthong is [ʊ], <u>not</u> [u] as in *too*. The lips are rounded, but the rounding is not so small for [ʊ] as for [u]. [ɑu] would be an exaggeration.

Practice singing:

now	town	thou	about	
vow	frown	thousand	shout	
how	crowd	found	proud	bough
plow	brown	round	shroud	
brow	allow	ground	crouch	

Examples in vocal texts:

O th*ou* that tellest good tidings to Zion . . . (*Messiah;* Handel)
Though th*ou* the waters warp . . .
　　　　　(*Blow, Blow, Thou Winter Wind;* Shakespeare, Quilter)
My shr*ou*d of white, stuck all with yew . . .
A th*ou*sand, th*ou*sand sighs to save . . .
　　　　　(*Come Away, Death;* Shakespeare, Quilter)
Loveliest of trees, the cherry n*ow*
Is hung with bloom along the b*ou*gh.
　　　　　　(*Loveliest of Trees;* Housman, Duke)
All of us, ev'ryone of us has something to sing ab*ou*t,
To sing and sh*ou*t.
　　　　　(*Holiday Song;* Taggard, William Schuman)

[oʊ] AS IN *No*

The phonetic symbols [oʊ] represent the diphthong that is the vowel sound in the word *no*. It is composed of [o], as in the unstressed syllable of *obey*, plus [ʊ], as in *full*. Examples of other spellings of this diphthong: *soul, though, know, road, sew, doe, owe, Oh, O.*

The sound of *o* is always diphthongized in English when it appears in:

1) Words or exclamations of one syllable (*no, road, grow, Oh, O,* etc.)
2) Words of more than one syllable where it receives any stress whatever (*lonely,* hearth*stone,* de*vo*tion, con*so*ling, bar*carolle,* mari*gold,* etc.)

Only when it is completely unstressed is it pronounced with merely one vowel (*obey, memory,* etc., see Chapter 38).

While we all, without realizing it, pronounce a diphthong for stressed *o* when we speak, many people sing this diphthong incorrectly, omitting the second vowel. When the word is sustained for a longer duration in singing than it is in speech, the singer, unaware that he diphthongizes it in speaking, somehow neglects to add the second vowel.

Many a singer who pronounces *I don't know, do not go, lonely, snow,* etc., correctly in speaking, somehow introduces an *aw* sound, pronouncing these words as "I dawn't knaw," "do not gaw," "lawnly," "snaw," etc., in singing. Like the man who did not know that he had been speaking prose all his life, the singer may not be conscious that he has been using diphthongs for years. Once he recognizes a diphthong as such, and gets on singing as well as speaking terms with it, he will no longer disregard its presence and when he sings "I love you so," he will not startle his audience by proclaiming, "I love you, saw."

Therefore, it is important to identify both vowels and to pronounce both correctly.

SHAPE OF LIPS

The diphthong [oʊ] must be started with large rounded lips which become medium-rounded at its termination. This is important.

Let us review the three vowels that require lip-rounding:

[o] is large;
[ʊ] is medium;
[u] is small.

[oʊ] employs the first two vowels.

Do not use the small lip-rounding of [u] in the diphthong [oʊ]. As a first vowel, it would result in distortion (*goo hoom* for *go home*); as a second vowel, it would result in another distortion, giving the effect of singing through a mouthful of food. It is a common fault among singers to start this diphthong with medium-rounded lips [ʊ]. It is then difficult to make the lips smaller for the second vowel, and the diphthong loses intelligibility and brilliance of tone.

Practice singing:

no	home	soul	know	devotion
go	tone	though	glow	consoling
so	rose	road	blow	marigold
ago	alone	roam	sew	barcarolle
lo!	old	foam	sorrow	
Oh	rode	foe	window	poem ⎤
O	awoke	woe	meadow	poet ⎦ 1st syllable

Examples in vocal texts:

Behold, and see if there be any sorrow like unto his sorrow.

(Messiah; Handel)

Go, lovely rose . . .

(Waller, Quilter)

O that it were so . . .

(Landor, Bridge)

Wealth I seek not, hope nor love,
Nor a friend to know me;
All I seek, the heaven above,
And the road below me.

(The Vagabond; Stevenson, Vaughan Williams)

47. DIPHTHONGS AND TRIPHTHONGS ENDING IN THE NEUTRAL VOWEL

A triphthong is a sound composed of three consecutive vowels in the same syllable. There are four diphthongs and two triphthongs ending in the neutral vowel.

Diphthong		Key Word
[ɛə]	as in	*air*
[ɪə]	as in	*ear*
[ɔə]	as in	*ore*
[ʊə]	as in	*sure*
Triphthong		
[ɑɪə]	as in	*ire*
[ɑʊə]	as in	*our*

Memorize the key words. They can be remembered easily if they are associated with the five vowel letters of the alphabet:

A for *air*
E for *ear*
I for *ire* (triphthong)
O for *ore*
U for *sure*
. . . . *our* (the second triphthong in the list has no alphabetical letter with which it can be associated readily)

It can be observed that all of the words having these diphthongs are spelled with final *r* or *re*, and in each, the *r* or *re* is replaced by the neutral vowel.

174

In these diphthongs, as in all others, the first vowel is sustained, and the second vowel is added at the very end. In the two triphthongs, also, the first vowel is sustained. The last two vowels are added at the very end.

There is even less contrast between the vowel sounds within these diphthongs (and triphthongs) than between those within the previous five diphthongs, and the change from one vowel to the next is even more subtle.

[εə] AS IN *Air*

The phonetic symbols [εə] represent the diphthong that, in singing, constitutes the word *air*. It is composed of [ε], as in *wed*, plus [ə], the neutral vowel, which replaces the *r*. Examples of other spellings of this diphthong: *dare, where, bear, their, e'er, prayer.*

First, sing [ε] with relaxed, dropped lower lip. At the very end of the syllable, the [ε] changes, almost imperceptibly, to [ə]. Do not exaggerate the second vowel by singing it as *ah* or *uh*.

Avoid the error of singing [εɪ] plus the neutral vowel. Sing only [ε] plus the neutral vowel.

Practice singing:

air	dare	there	their
fair	care	where	heir
chair	fare		
hair	rare	bear	e'er
lair	share	pear	ne'er
pair	compare	tear (verb)	
despair	declare	wear	prayer

Examples in vocal texts:
My lovely Celia, heav'nly *fair;*
As lilies sweet, as soft as *air.*
                    (*My Lovely Celia;* George Monro)

My mother bids me bind my *hair*
With bands of rosy hue,
Tie up my sleeves with ribands *rare*
And lace my bodice blue.
                    (*My Mother Bids Me Bind My Hair;* Haydn)

r IS ADDED TO DIPHTHONG WHEN FOLLOWED BY VOWEL

Before a consonant or a pause, the sound of the diphthong is [ɛə] without an *r;* but when the next syllable or word begins with a vowel, an *r* is added to the diphthong, in accordance with the rule that *r* must always be sung before a vowel. (See page 13.) For example, *airy* is pronounced [ɛərɪ] because final *y* is a vowel; *air in* is pronounced [ɛərɪn].

When adding *r,* do not omit the diphthong. Contrast the following words:

Diphthong plus *r*	[ɛ] plus *r*
vary [vɛərɪ]	very [vɛrɪ]
dairy [dɛərɪ]	derry [dɛrɪ]
Mary [mɛərɪ]	merry [mɛrɪ]

The phrase "Where e'er you walk" is a good illustration of the diphthong with and without an added *r.* The first word, *where,* has the diphthong plus *r* because it is followed by *e'er* which begins with a vowel. *E'er* has merely the diphthong, with no *r* added, because it is followed by *you* which begins with a consonant. (*y* at the beginning of a syllable is a consonant.)

Where e'er you walk is sung: [hwɛərɛə] *you walk.*

Practice singing:

airy	despairing	fairer	share it
vary	daring	rarest	glare of noon
dairy	declaring	declareth	there it is

Examples in vocal texts:

And cry unto her that her war*fare* is accomplished.

(*Messiah;* Handel)

My shroud of white, stuck all with yew,
O pre*pare* it!
My part of death, no one so true
Did *share* it.   (*Come Away, Death;* Shakespeare, Quilter)
Take a *pair* of sparkling eyes . . . (*The Gondoliers;* Gilbert and
Sullivan)

[ɪə] AS IN *Ear*

The phonetic symbols [ɪə] represent the diphthong that constitutes the word *ear*. It is composed of [ɪ], as in *it*, plus [ə], the neutral
vowel, which replaces the *r*. Examples of other spellings of this diphthong: *here, cheer, tier, weir, hero, we're.*

Special warning: do not sing [i], as in *me*, as the first vowel of
this diphthong; sing [ɪ], as in *it.*

Practice singing:

ear	clear	here	cheer	tier
dear	appear	mere	deer	pier
fear	endear	austere	beer	bier
hear	fearful	revere	leer	weir
near	tearful	sincere	sneer	we're

Examples in vocal texts:
I'll charm your willing *ears*
With songs of lovers' *fears,*
While sympathetic *tears*
My cheeks bedew.
> (*A Wand'ring Minstrel,* from *The Mikado;* Gilbert and Sul-
> livan)

Though related to a *peer,*
I can hand, reef and *steer* . . .
Then give three *cheers* and one *cheer* more . . .
> (*I Am the Captain of the Pinafore,* from *H.M.S. Pinafore;*
> Gilbert and Sullivan)

Remember to add *r* to the diphthong when it is followed by a
vowel. (See page 176.)

Practice singing:

dearest	cheerily	here it is
dreary	hero	fear of death
appearance	mysterious	near us

Dearest, there to dream of thee . . .
And I watch the woods grow darker,
Hear the reeds' *mysterious* sighs . . .
> (*By a Lonely Forest Pathway;* transl. Chapman, Griffes)

[ɔə] AS IN *Ore*

The phonetic symbols [ɔə] represent the diphthong that constitutes the word *ore*. It is composed of [ɔ], as in *warm*, plus [ə], the neutral vowel, which replaces the *r*. Examples of other spellings of this diphthong: *four, floor, soar, o'er, you're*.

The following words should have the same diphthong [ɔə]:
    yore
    your
    yours
    you're

Even though the dictionary pronunciation for the last three may be *oor* [ʊə], usage has made it [ɔə], which is the pronunciation generally heard from accomplished speakers, actors, and singers. It is a more euphonious sound than *yoor*. This modification of the vowel does not, of course, extend to *you*, whose *oo* sound [u] is not subject to change.

Among the words represented by the diphthong [ɔə], there is a strange but common error: many singers confuse *pour* and *poor*. *Pour* should be pronounced [pɔə]. *Poor* should be pronounced [pʊə] (see next diphthong). Memory aid: when pronouncing *pour*, think of *more*.

Practice singing:

ore	adore	four	roar
more	before	your	soar
shore	implore	yours	floor
wore	restore	you're	door
yore	evermore	pour	o'er

Examples in vocal texts:
    Ye people, rend *your* hearts, and not *your* garments, for *your* transgressions . . . If with all *your* hearts . . .
                                        (*Elijah;* Mendelssohn)
    And take from seventy springs a *score*,
    It only leaves me fifty *more*.
                                (*Loveliest of Trees;* Housman, Duke)
    Go 'way from my window,
    Go 'way from my *door*.   (John Jacob Niles)

Remember to add *r* to the diphthong when it is followed by a vowel. (See page 176.)

Practice singing:

adoring	glory	adore it	four angels
moreover	story	before us	your eyes

And the *glory* of the Lord shone round about them, and they were *sore* afraid.   (*Messiah;* Handel)

THE PREPOSITION *for*
THE CONJUNCTIONS *or* AND *nor*

In accordance with the principle that prepositions and conjunctions receive no stress, the preposition *for* and the conjunctions *or* and *nor* are not diphthongized, because they would automatically become emphasized. Sing them with the single vowel [ɔ].

Note the difference between single vowel and diphthong in the following:

Single Vowel [ɔ]   Diphthong [ɔə]

for brothers   four brothers
the sky or the sea   the sky o'er the sea

[ʊə] AS IN *Sure*

The phonetic symbols [ʊə] represent the diphthong that is the vowel sound in the word *sure*. It is composed of [ʊ], as in *full* plus [ə], the neutral vowel, which replaces the *r*.

Examples of other spellings of this diphthong: *tour, poor.*

Be sure to start this diphthong with the vowel [ʊ], as in *full*, not with the vowel [u], as in *too*. The lips should have the medium-rounded shape of [ʊ], not the smallest rounded shape of [u].

Here, it seems pertinent to recall to your attention that *poor* has the diphthong [ʊə], and to add to the memory aid begun in connection with *pour* [ɔə]: To pour more is a poor cure. There is another perhaps painfully picturesque way to remember which word is which: there are two zeros in *poor!*

In many [ʊə] words, a *y* sound precedes the diphthong (*pure, cure,* etc.). The *y* is considered a consonant, like the *y* at the beginning of a syllable, and has no effect upon the diphthong.

Practice singing:

sure	endure	poor
pure	allure	boor
cure	secure	moor
lure	demure	tour
assure	obscure	dour

Examples in vocal texts:

Ye shall ever *surely* find me . . .   (*Elijah;* Mendelssohn)
Love that no wrong can *cure* . . .
That is the love that's *pure* . . .
Love that will aye *endure*.

(*Love Is a Plaintive Song,* from *Patience;* Gilbert and Sullivan)

Remember to add *r* to the diphthong when it is followed by a vowel.

Practice singing:

curious	sure of
enduring	pure in heart

Diphthongs occur only in stressed syllables. Note the difference between the words *assure* and *pressure.* In *assure,* the second syllable is stressed and has a diphthong; in *pressure,* it is unstressed and has a neutral vowel. In words like *pleasure* and *measure,* many singers who doubtless pronounce the second syllable correctly with a neutral vowel when they speak, mispronounce it by using a diphthong when they sing.

Here is a representative list of such words. Be sure to pronounce the unstressed syllables with a neutral vowel, and not with a diphthong.

Practice singing:

pleasure	nature	feature
measure	rapture	creature
treasure	capture	venture
leisure	future	lecture

TRIPHTHONGS

[ɑɪə] AS IN *Ire*

The phonetic symbols [ɑɪə] represent the triphthong that constitutes the word *ire*. The letter *i*, in this case, spells a sound composed
of two vowels: [ɑ], as in *ah*, plus [ɪ], as in *it*. Therefore, *ire* is composed of three vowels: [ɑɪ] plus the neutral vowel [ə], which replaces
the *r*.

Examples of other spellings of this triphthong: *lyre, briar, choir.*

In singing triphthongs, the first vowel is sustained (just as in
diphthongs) and the last two vowels are added at the very end.
When the triphthong occurs on more than one note, the first vowel
is sustained on all the notes and the last two vowels are added at
the very end of the last note.

To illustrate, the word *fire* is sung as follows:

Practice singing on one note; then on two or three notes:

ire	dire	desire	lyre
fire	mire	inspire	briar
sire	tire	conspire	choir

Examples in vocal texts:
Is not His word like a *fire?* . . . I *desire* to live no longer . . .

(*Elijah;* Mendelssohn)

Small is the worth
Of beauty from the light *retired;*
Bid her come forth,
Suffer herself to be *desired,*
And not blush so to be *admired.*

(*Go, Lovely Rose;* Waller, Quilter)

When followed by a vowel sound, the *r* is, of course, added to
the triphthong.

Practice singing:
retiring   The fire is blazing.
conspiring   They inspire us.

[ɑʊə] AS IN *Our*

The phonetic symbols [ɑʊə] represent the triphthong that constitutes the word *our*. The letters *ou* in this case spell a sound composed of two vowels: [ɑ], as in *ah*, plus [ʊ], as in *full*. Therefore, *our* is composed of three vowels: [ɑʊ] plus the neutral vowel [ə], which replaces the *r*.

Example of another spelling of this triphthong: *flower*.

Words with this triphthong may be spelled with *-our* or with *-ower*, and their pronunciation is identical. For example, *flour* and *flower* are alike in pronunciation. They should be sung in exactly the same manner: that is, as a triphthong, sustaining the first vowel [ɑ], and adding the last two vowels at the very end, in this manner:

[flɑ - ʊə]

When one of these words occurs on more than one note, sing the first vowel on all the notes, adding the last two vowels at the very end of the last note, in this manner:

[flɑ - ʊə]   [flɑ - - - ʊə]

Avoid the division of *-ower* words into two syllables, even though such a separation may be indicated in type. It is common practice for a word like *flower*, for instance, to be printed as *flow-er* with *flow* under one note and *er* under the next; but to sing the word as if. it were two syllables results in something callow, prosy, and "square." Careful treatment of [ɑʊə] is one of the marks of artistry in diction. In the expert translation by Robert A. Simon of Ravel's *L'Heure Espagnole*, the tenor who plays the role of the fatuous poet has been equipped with many *flower-shower-bower* rhymes, which fall on expansive intervals in a habanera rhythm. When he (intentionally, of course) sings these words as *flow-wah, show-wah,* and *bow-wah,* it is with comic effect and draws appreciative laughter from the audience. But an artist singing a serious song in a serious recital would experience a shock to hear giggles from his listeners.

Be sure to sing [ʊ] as the second vowel in the triphthong. Do not sing [u], for the *w* effect would be emphasized.

Practice singing, first on one note, then on more than one:

our	flower	cower
hour	bower	dower
flour	power	glower
devour	shower	tower

Examples in vocal texts:

To his music plants and *flowers*
Ever sprung; as sun and *showers*
There had made a lasting spring.
(*Orpheus with His Lute;* Shakespeare, William Schuman)
Oh, clasp we to *our* hearts, for deathless *dower,*
That close-companioned inarticulate *hour* . . .
(*Silent Noon;* Rossetti, Vaughan Williams)

When followed by a vowel, the *r* is, as usual, added to the triphthong.

Practice singing:

devouring	my hour of need
overpowering	a flower in the field

DIPHTHONGS AND TRIPHTHONGS ON HIGH NOTES
BEFORE A PAUSE

It has been pointed out that in the diphthongs and triphthongs spelled with final *r* or final *re,* the neutral vowel replaces the *r.* This is the pronunciation before a consonant or a pause.

But now we arrive at an exception: When one of these diphthongs or triphthongs spelled with final *r* or *re* occurs before a pause on an extremely high note, the *r* may be restored, and the neutral vowel eliminated.

The reason for this will be obvious if you will make the following experiments: Sing a phrase ending in *fire* [fɑɪə] (*my heart is on fire*) with the last word on a very high note. The neutral vowel will sound like a huge *yah.* Now sing the same phrase, ending on the same high note, without the neutral vowel of *fire.* The result will be *fie* [fɑɪ] which is incomplete. Finally, sing the same phrase on the same high note with a slightly flipped *r* in place of the neutral vowel. This will solve the difficulty. This small flipped *r* on the high note will be entirely unobjectionable.

This is the exception mentioned in the Second Basic Rule of *r*. (See page 13.)

Remember:
1) that this is necessary only on very high notes;
2) that this is necessary only before a pause
   (when followed by a consonant, *r* is omitted, and when followed by a vowel sound, *r* is added to the diphthong);
3) that it is only in <u>diphthongs</u> and <u>triphthongs</u> spelled with final *r* or *re* that the *r* is sung. In a word having a single vowel (such as *star, far, are, ever, never,* etc.) no *r* is needed before a pause, no matter how high the note.

48. WHEN TO SING [æ]; WHEN TO SING *AH*

The majority of words spelled with *a* have the sound of [æ], as in *cat*. In words like *hand, glad, happy, man, shadow, vanish,* and hundreds more, the only correct and acceptable vowel sound of the accented syllable is [æ]. For convenience, we shall call these the "hand words."

There is a smaller group of words in which *a* may be pronounced in one of two ways: as [æ] by most Americans; as "broad *ah*" by some Americans and by the British. This group, which includes *ask, dance, laugh, pass, last,* etc., is frequently called the "ask words," for quick identification. (Such words as *father, heart, start, part, calm,* etc., are not included in this category. They are *ah* words which never are pronounced with any other vowel. Only words in which a choice is made between [æ] and *ah* are *ask* words.)

Many singers indulge in the unfortunate habit of substituting *ah* for [æ] in *hand* words. Such malpronunciations as *hahnd, glahd, hahppy, mahn,* to select only a few, sound pretentious, arty, and absurd to an audience. (Many network producers frown on what are known as "shahdow and vahnish singers.") Substitution of *ah* for [æ] in *hand* words is a symptom of faulty technique, carelessness, or affectation.

Let us examine the three causes of the undesirable pronunciation of *ah* in the *hand* words:

FAULTY TECHNIQUE. Because singers seldom vocalize on [æ], many of them do not develop the ability to sing this sound with beauty of tone. Their consequent insecurity in the production of [æ] prompts them to fear and avoid it. Suggested remedy: Vocalize on [æ].

CARELESSNESS. Some singers fail to listen to the sounds they make, and, even with the most virtuous of intentions, substitute *ah* for [æ] inadvertently. Suggested remedy: Listen to your vowels.

AFFECTATION. Many singers, having heard that the broad *ah* is the correct vowel for certain words in cultivated pronunciation, conclude that this *ah* must be sung exclusively in the interests of refinement. When they lavish *ah* on *hand* instead of singing the authentic [æ], they affect a pronunciation that is not genuine — or that is, to use a good professional adjective for it, phoney. Suggested remedy. Learn which words are which.

How to Know Which Words Are Which

It would be an excessive task to memorize the words in both groups. It is more efficient to classify the groups on the basis of the consonant that follows the letter *a*.

Below is a list of the consonants that determine the *hand* words. It will be obvious that memorization of these consonants would be almost as burdensome as memorizing the words themselves. This will not be necessary. But we present the list of consonants along with a few examples of the words to indicate their wide scope.

EXAMPLES OF *hand* WORDS

	-b	stab, rabble, cabin
	-c	accent, act
	-ck	back, attack, lack
	-d	glad, sad, shadow, mad, had
	-g	magic, dagger, wagon
	-l	hallowed, valley, shall
Stressed *a*	-m	am, lamb, lamp, camp
is pronounced	-n	man, can, cannot, vanish
[æ]	-nd	hand, band, grand, land, stand
when followed	-ng	anguish, languish, sang, language
by these	-nk	thank, sank, drank
consonants	-p	happy, capture, rapture
	-sh	clash, dash, fashion, flash
	-t	cat, matter, that (demonstrative)
	-tch	catch, latch, match
	-v	have, ravish, lavish, savage
	-x	wax, relax, axe
	-z	dazzle, hazard

It will be easier to memorize the far shorter list of consonants that determine the *ask* words. To facilitate still further the learning of these consonants, we shall list the consonantal <u>sounds</u>, rather than the actual spellings:

SOUNDS DETERMINING THE *ask* WORDS

Stressed *a*		*f*	(in all the spellings of this sound)
may be pronounced		*nce*	(and the same sound spelled -*ns*)
ah		*nch*	
when followed by		*s*	
these sounds		*th*	
		and a few special -*mand* and -*nt* words	

Examples of the *ask* words, and exceptions, will be given in the charts on pages 188 and 190.

LIMITED USE OF *ah* IN SINGING *ask* WORDS

Before studying the charts that exemplify the *ask* words, it must be pointed out that these words are sung with the *ah* pronunciation only when they appear in the types of music in which the flipped *r* is used; namely:

1. Opera

2. Sacred Music and Art Songs

3. Works that Require a British Accent

All other types of music are sung with the American *r* — and with the [æ] pronunciation for *ask* words.

DIRECTIONS FOR STUDY OF THE *ask* WORDS: CHART I

1. Memorize the consonantal sounds in the left-hand column. These are the sounds, not spellings, of consonants following stressed *a* which determine the *ask* words.

2. Note well the examples of *ask* words in the central column.

3. Memorize the exceptions in the right-hand column. These words must be pronounced with [æ].

4. Remember that any consonantal sounds that do not appear in the left-hand column occur in *hand* words [æ], which need not be memorized because they are too numerous.

SOUNDS AFTER LETTER *a*	EXAMPLES OF *ask* WORDS (*ah*)			EXCEPTIONS* [æ]
-f (in all spellings)	laugh draught calf half	after draft shaft waft	chaff quaff staff	baffle daffodil scaffold
-nce (and same sound spelled *-ns*) *-nch*	dance chance glance France	prance trance advance entrance (verb) branch blanch avalanche	answer trans- (prefix)	fancy romance circumstance expanse

-s	brass
	class
	
	ask
	bask
	basket
	clasp
	gasp
	aghast
	blast
	cast
	disaster
	fast
		glass
		grass
		pass
		
		cask
		casket
		flask
		
		ghastly
		mast
		master
		vast
			castle
			fasten
			
			mask
			rascal
			task
			grasp
			rasp
			passed
			past
			pastime
			pastor
			repast
				classic
				passage
				passenger
				
				(*z* sound)
				  as, has
				  chasm
				
				(*sh* sound)
				  passion
				  compassion
				
				cascade
				
				aspect
				
				hast
				chastise
				fantastic

-th	bath path		rather wrath	gather hath, fathom

CHART I

---

*Additional exceptions which rarely occur in vocal literature have been omitted here. For reference, see Appendix 2 (page 198).

SPECIAL NOTE ON *-n* AND *-sh*

Observe that *n* alone and *sh* are not included among the consonantal sounds that determine the *ask* words. *Can, man, plan,* etc. and *crash, flash, fashion,* etc., are *hand* words [æ].

FIVE MOST IMPORTANT EXCEPTIONS

fancy
romance
circumstance
expanse
gather

The five exceptions given above are tremendously important, especially the first two, which appear frequently in vocal literature. They must be established unquestionably in the singer's mind as [æ] words.

MEMORY AIDS FOR LEARNING THE EXCEPTIONS

All forms of *have* are [æ] words: *hast, has, hath.*
All derivatives of *fancy* are [æ] words: *fanciful, fantastic, fantasy.*
Answer (ah) is the logical reply to *ask (ah).*

SUFFIXES AND INFLECTED ENDINGS DO NOT CHANGE *ask* WORDS

Suffixes (*-ment,* etc.) and inflected endings (*-ed, -es, -ing,* etc.) do not change the essential vowel sounds of words. Look at the following word sequences by way of illustration:

ask words	[æ] words
advance, advancement	fancy, fancied, fancies
pass, passed, passes, passing	romance, romances

RHYME DOES NOT AFFECT *ask* WORDS AND THEIR EXCEPTIONS

You will find a detailed discussion of the problem of rhymes in our next chapter. But we shall anticipate it briefly here by noting that rhyming has no effect whatsoever on *ask* words and their exceptions. In music to which it is appropriate, an *ask* word is always an *ask* word, and an exception is always pronounced with [æ].

CONCERNING CHART II

Now we turn to Chart II, which comprises words having the letter *a* followed by *-nd* and *-nt*. Here the exceptions outnumber the *ask* words to such an extent that we have listed. the *ask* words completely, in the second column. These should be memorized. All other -*and* and -*ant* words must have [æ].

DIRECTIONS FOR STUDY OF *ask* WORDS: CHART II

1. Memorize the consonantal sounds in the left-hand column.
2. Memorize the *ask* words in the central column.
3. Remember that all other -*and* and -*ant* words have the [æ] sound.

SOUNDS AFTER LETTER *a*	*ask* WORDS THESE WORDS ONLY (*ah*)	[æ] WORDS
-*nd*	command demand countermand reprimand	All other -*and* words
-*nt*	can't (with apostrophe) shan't (with apostrophe) aunt advantage chant enchant grant plant slant	All other -*ant* words

CHART II

As usual, suffixes and inflected endings do not change the essential vowel sounds of words. As illustration, the second syllables of the following are not affected by their various endings:

enchant, enchants, enchanted, enchanting, enchantment
command, commands, commanded, commanding, commandment

THE INCONSISTENCY OF MAN

It is an odd commentary on the inconsistency of man that the very singer who demurs at singing the [æ] sound where it is absolutely obligatory, and argues that he cannot sing it, will blissfully sing [æ] in a word like *enchant,* in an art song where *ah* would be preferable. And vice versa, the singer who cannot see why he should sing *ah* in *enchant* in an art song, will sing *hahnd,* which he should never do in any music.

Examples of *hand* words [æ] in vocal texts:

And he shall *gather* the *lambs* with his arm . . .

(Messiah, Handel)

On the *bat's back* I do fly . . .

(Where the Bee Sucks; Shakespeare, Arne)

Take a figure trimly *planned* . . .
Take a tender little *hand* . . .
Ah! Take all these, you lucky *man* —
Take and keep them if you *can.*

(Take a Pair of Sparkling Eyes, from The Gondoliers; Gilbert and Sullivan)

Examples of *ask* words (*ah*) in appropriate vocal texts:

I know a green *grass path* . . .

(The Green River; Douglas, Carpenter)

And I have seen your fingers hold this *glass.*
These things do not remember you, beloved,
And yet your touch upon them will not *pass.*

(Music I Heard with You; Aiken, Hageman)

Examples of both *hand* words and *ask* words in vocal texts:

My *Master* (*ah*) *hath* [æ] a garden . . .

(Poem anon., Thompson)

Would I might *clasp* (*ah*) them, the whole creation,
With fervent *rapture* [æ] to my heart.

(Pilgrim's Song; transl. England, Tchaikovsky)

The phrases of the *past* (*ah*) anew I try to *fashion* [æ],
I whisper and recall the words that voiced our *passion* [æ] . . .

(The Silence of the Night; transl. Harris, Jr. and Taylor, Rachmaninoff)

In the fell clutch of circumstance [æ] . . .
Under the bludgeonings of chance (*ah*) . . .

(Invictus; Henley, Huhn)

49. TO RHYME OR NOT TO RHYME

The Word *Again* Always Rhymes

The word *again* has two pronunciations. The prevalent pronunciation of the second syllable is *gayn* [geɪn] in Britain, and *gen* [gɛn] in America. But when there is no definitely national characteristic in the text, you may follow your own choice. But because *again* has two legitimate pronunciations, when the poet obviously intended it to rhyme, LET 'ER RHYME! For example, when *again* is coupled with *rain*, it is *agayn;* when it is paired with *then*, it is *agen*.
Examples in vocal texts:

Ah, Moon of my Delight, that knows no *wane*,
The Moon of Heav'n is rising once *again* . . . (*agayn*)
> (*In a Persian Garden;* transl. Fitzgerald, Lehmann)
But keep the wolf far thence that's known to *men*,
For with his nails he'll dig them up *again*. (*agen*)
> (*Dirge;* Webster, Virgil Thomson)

Wind: A Special Case

In earlier English, the noun *wind* had the vowel sound of the word *mind*. It is traditional to give it this pronunciation when the rhyme demands it, but only in early English poetry.
Examples:

Blow, blow, thou winter *wind,*
Thou art not so *unkind* . . .   (Shakespeare, Quilter)
O! Then if she remain still so *unkind,*
I may as well complain unto the *wind*.
> (*Cease, O My Sad Soul;* Purcell)
In works of a later time, the vowel sound should be [ɪ] as in *window*, no matter what the rhyme.

Other Words May Not Be Changed for the Sake of a Rhyme

Other words must be sung with their normal pronunciations even when rhymed with words that sound different. You may find *some* as the rhyming partner for *home*, for example, but do not try to equalize the sounds. Such rhymes are "eye rhymes." An eye rhyme, which is a legitimate feature in versification, matches words that look alike, although they do not sound alike. In singing, pronounce each word correctly, regardless of the rhyme.

Examples:

love	earth	dance (*ah*)
prove	hearth	romance [æ]

deny [ɑɪ]	paradise (ends in *s*)
destiny [ɪ]	eyes (ends in *z*)

50. A LAST WORD: PATTER

DESPARD
MURGATROYD: If I had been so lucky as to have a steady brother
Who could talk to me as we are talking now to one
another —
Who could give me good advice when he discovered
I was erring
(Which is just the very favour which on you I am
conferring),
My story would have made a rather interesting idyll,
And I might have lived and died a very decent
indiwiddle.
This particularly rapid, unintelligible patter

ROBIN
OAKAPPLE: Isn't generally heard, and if it is, it doesn't matter!
If it is, it doesn't matter —

MAD MARGARET: If it ain't, it doesn't matter —

ALL: If it is, it doesn't matter, matter, matter, matter,
matter!

(*Ruddigore,* Act II)

"As we are talking now to one another" (and I intend no implications from the first six lines of Despard), perhaps I may give you some good advice when you must sing a song like the excerpt from *Ruddigore.* The particularly rapid patter must be heard, and it must <u>seem</u> to be intelligible. Sir W. S. Gilbert, I'm sure, never wrote a line that he didn't want to be understood; and when they are sung by accomplished dictioners, the words constantly step up and shake hands with the audience. Even the flashing sequences in patter songs. The trick is not to try to make a Big Thing of articulating laboriously every syllable, or to cheat both Gilbert and Sullivan by slowing down the tempo. All you need to do is concentrate on the principal words or syllables in each phrase, subordinating the others so that the public will say: "I understood every word." It's an aural illusion that you can master with a little practice. If you were to pop each syllable out perfectly on the same plane with every other one, the listener wouldn't be so impressed. He'd say: "It's too fast for me." This reaction, too, is part of the aural illusion. That which sounds natural is understood.

And this last word on patter — which I hope you will hear, because I think it matters — is a tiny but basic summary of all that we have tried to accomplish since we first looked at the silent letters on page 6. If your diction sounds natural — if it is simply the vehicle by which you express words and music so that your listener notices only what is being said in text and tone and isn't aware that any diction rules, devices, or suggestions are being used — your diction is good. That's what this book has hoped to do: to provide for you a method of articulation that will make your articulation so persuasive that no one will be conscious of method. It may seem a bit pretentious to allude to the saying about the art that conceals art. And yet — for the artist, diction is an art.

Au revoir — Artist!

APPENDIX 1

Reference list of [ɔ] words. (See Chapter 39.)

Spellings: *al* (also *ald, alk, all, alt*)
au
aught
aw
ought

Special words: *water, broad* (and its derivatives)
broth, froth, wroth

al	*all*	*alt*	*au* (cont.)	*au* (cont.)
almost	ball	altar	assault	inaugurate
also	befall	alter	autumn	jaunt
although	call	exalt	bauble	jaunty
always	caller	falter	because	laud
appal	enthrall	Gibraltar	cause	launch
falcon	fall	halt	caution	maraud
stalwart	hall	halter	cautious	Paul
withal	install	malt	clause	paunch
	mall	psalter	daub	pauper
ald	recall	salt	daunt	pause
	small		default	plaudit
bald	squall	*au*	exhaust	precaution
scald	stall		faun	raucous
	tall	auburn	fault	Saul
alk	thrall	audacious	gaudy	sauce
	wall	audience	gaunt	saucy
*balk		audition	gauntlet	taut
*chalk		augur	gauze	vault
*stalk		August	haul	
*talk		applaud	haunch	
*walk		applause	holocaust	

---

*The *l* is silent.

aught	*aw*	*aw* (cont.)	*ought*	*Miscellaneous*
caught	awe	hawthorn	besought	water
daughter	awful	jaw	brought	broad (also
distraught	bawl	law	fought	broaden,
fraught	brawl	lawn	ought	abroad, etc.)
haughty	brawn	overawe	sought	broth
naught	brawny	raw	thought	froth
naughty	claw	saw	trough	wroth
onslaught	crawl	scrawl		
slaughter	daw	scrawny		
taught	dawn	shawl		
	dawdle	squaw		
	draw	squawk		
	drawl	tawdry		
	drawn	tawny		
	flaw	thaw		
	gnaw	withdraw		
	hawk	yawn		

APPENDIX 2

Supplementary list of exceptions to *ask* words. (See page 188.)

All words in this chart must be pronounced with [æ].

-f	-nce	-nch	-s		-th
gaff	cancel	franchise	classify	asperity	
gaffer	finance		crass	aspic	
graphic	stance		cuirass	aspirate	
riffraff			gas	Caspian	
traffic			morass		
			passive	asterisk	*math* (as any
			mascot	bombast	syllable of
			Alaska	castigate	a word)
			gasket	drastic	
				plastic	
				sarcastic	
				spastic	

The following words may be pronounced either with [æ] or *ah:*

alas	enhance
ant	exasperate
asp	lass
aspen	mass
ass	masquerade
aster	mastiff
blaspheme	pasture
contrast	plantation
elastic	ranch